Canadian Christian Zionism

Canadian Christian Zionism
A Tangled Tale

Ron Dart

Synaxis Press

Synaxis Press

CANADIAN CHRISTIAN ZIONISM
A Tangled Tale

Copyright © 2015 Synaxis Press. All rights reserved. No portion of this book may be reproduced, stored in a retrieval system or transmitted in any form by any means—electronic, mechanical, photocopy, recording, scanning or other—except for brief quotations in critical reviews or articles, without prior written permission of the publisher.

Synaxis Press
Dewdney, BC, Canada

www.synaxispress.ca

ISBN-13:
ISBN-10:

Cataloguing-in-Publication Data:

Canadian christian zionism : a tangled tale / Ron Dart

xx + 110 p. ; 21 cm. Including bibliographical references.

ISBN-13:

1. Political Science 2. Canadian History. I. Dart, Ron 1950–. II. Title.

Manufactured in Canada

This book is dedicated to all those men, women, and children (past, present, and future) who, like the dove, seek peace between Christians, Jews, and Muslims in a just and wise, dialogical and co-existing manner. And, to Martin Buber and Judah Magnes, who walked the prophetic narrow ridge.

Now, the wars they will be fought again,
The Holy Dove—She will be caught again,
Bought and sold and bought again,
The Dove is never free.
Ring the bells that still can ring,
Forget your perfect offering.
There is a crack, a crack in everything,
That's how the light gets in.

—Leonard Cohen, "Anthem"

I dreamed kind Jesus fouled the big-gun gears;
And caused a permanent stoppage in all bolts;
And buckled with a smile Mausers and Colts;
And rusted every bayonet with His tears.

—Wilfred Owen, "Soldier's Dream"

Contents

Acknowledgements / xiii

Preface / xiv

1. A Tangled Tale / 1

2. Dawn of the Dilemma / 6

3. Canadian Academics and Christian Zionism / 17

4. Biblical Exegesis and Christian Zionism / 23

5. The Conservative Party and Christian Zionism / 37

6. Populist Evangelicals and Christian Zionism / 41

7. Conclusion / 47

   Appendix I: George Grant and *Exiles from Nowhere: The Jews and the Canadian Elite* / 50

   Appendix II: Martin Buber (1878–1965), Zionism, and the Prophetic / 55

Appendix III: Jesus, the Beatitudes, and the Prophetic / 61

Appendix IV: The Jewish Prophetic Tradition: Then and Now / 65

Appendix V: Irving Layton, Zionism, and the USA / 69

Afterword I: My History with Israel — Brad Jersak / 75

Afterword II: Abandoning Apocalyptic Determinism in Favour of Compassion for Palestinians
— Andrew P. Klager / 81

Afterword III: Christian Zionism
— Wayne Northey / 93

Afterword IV: Christian Zionism: An Eschatological Cult — Archbishop Lazar Puhalo / 100

Bibliography / 103

Acknowledgements

I would like to acknowledge Archbishop Lazar Puhalo who published the book, Andrew Klager who polished the text, Wayne Northey who mentioned the need, and Brad Jersak who has cheered such work on in the past via *Clarion Journal* and other publications.

And I would like to acknowledge *Sabeel* who, with the University of the Fraser Valley, hosted the first "Challenging Christian Zionism" conference on the West Coast in October 2014—may the April 2015 conference be a prophetic call to just peacemaking.

Preface

There has been a worrisome historic tendency within the academic disciplines of political science and religious studies to dwell in two solitudes. The political science tribe tend to be committed to the ethos of the secular and public realms and the religious studies clan has genuflected to the sacred and private environs—the former see the state as worthy of study, the latter the significance of society. This "never the twain shall meet" has harmed and hampered both intellectual disciplines.

There are hard empirical facts (explicit and implicit) that make it abundantly clear that there are a host of witnesses in the political realm that are deeply religious; hence, to ignore the deeper religious motivation that inspires political action is to be caught off guard when interpreting political positions taken by religious activists. The complex history of all the major and minor religions in the world can, when properly understood, assist those in the discipline of political science in making sense of why religious leaders take positions they do and why religious communities lean in certain directions on the hot button issues in the culture wars.

The dominance, myth, and hegemony of the secular paradigm and worldview developed for historic reasons, but such an approach, if taken with too much seriousness, tends to conceal and obscure a deeper and more persistent reality back of the secular. In short, the interest and engagement in the sacred is not likely to disappear or retreat into the private realms (although there are forms of religion and spirituality that do this).

I was quite fortunate in the 1990s to take a course with Martin Marty when he was in the midst (with Scott Appleby) of The Fundamentalist Project (that covered five volumes). The Fundamentalist Project lasted from 1991–1995, and the publication in 1992 of *The Glory and the Power: The Fundamentalist Challenge to the Modern World* made it more than obvious that there are those within religious communities that refuse to turn their backs on the public and political spheres of life.

Marty and Appleby touched down judiciously in this significant project on, obviously, right of centre tendencies in the secular-sacred divide, which had a tendency to reinforce the need to keep both areas of life separate. The Fundamentalist Project covered within the Western Tradition, Jewish, Christian, and Islamic fundamentalism, and within the Eastern Traditions, various forms of fundamentalism within these heritages; there was a fine chapter on Jewish fundamentalism and Christian Zionism in *The Glory and the Power*.

In the 1990s, Samuel Huntington published—initially in an article and then in a book—his clash of civilizations thesis. Huntington, in the post-1989 Cold War context, argued that the age of ideology was over and the global village would be entering a clash of civilizations era; Islam was seen as the primary threat to the West, and 9/11 seemed to reinforce Huntington's argument, but there could be no doubt that the integration of the secular and sacred was back on the table again. The debates and dialogue about 'clash of civilizations' and 'co-existence' of civilizations have been front and centre in the last decade.

The academic disciplines of political science and religious studies, like three-toed sloths, are slowly catching up to the reality that the sacred is not going to dissipate like a cloud in the sky, and many religious leaders and communities (for good or ill) will continue to enter the public and political realms—it is simply silly to ignore this persistent reality.

There are many areas of study that could be approached in the secular-sacred tension and reality, but I have chosen in this book to focus on Canadian Christian Zionism for a few reasons: first, there has been little work done in this area; second, Canadian Christian Zionism is part of the larger Christian Zionist tradition; third, the political aspects of Christian Zionism have serious implications for North America, the Middle East, and Palestinians; fourth, the present ruling party in Canada of Stephen Harper is one of the most Zionist in Canadian history.

I mentioned above the importance of understanding the relationship of the secular and sacred and the shift occurring that is open to uncovering what this means in political life. The publication of Marci McDonald's *The Armageddon Factor: The Rise of Christian Nationalism in Canada* in 2010 in many ways took Marty and Appleby's thesis and applied it to Canada. Marci did a couple of longer interviews with me for the weighty tome. There is an important chapter in the book that deals with Canadian Christian Zionism. The equally important publication of Dennis Greunding's *Pulpit and Politics: Competing Religious Ideologies in Canadian Public Life* (2011) also has significant chapters on Canadian Christian Zionism. Yves Engler has emerged in the last decade as the Noam Chomsky of Canada, and in his missive *Canada and Israel: Building Apartheid* (2010) he, in his fast paced way, brought to light many concealed facts about Canada and Israel.

There are those who will differ with Engler, but he is worth the read. The fact that Ronald Beiner (an important Canadian political philosopher) has turned to the secular-sacred issue in *Civil Religion: A Dialogue in the History of Political Philosophy* (2011) does need to be noted. The publication of Paul Rowe's *Religion and Global Politics* (2012) has, yet again, pondered the relationship between religion and politics from a more international perspective; there are chapters that deal with both Christian and Jewish Zionism in the book, although Canada is ignored.

I was fortunate as I was doing research for the book to have a lengthy phone conversation with Preston Manning. The Albertan religious-political tradition, as embodied by William Aberhart and Ernest Manning, has never veered far from the Christian-Jewish question and the relationship of the Jews to their historic homeland. The Aberhart era tended to be less sympathetic to the Jews (although the prophecy charts would point otherwise), whereas Ernest Manning had decidedly pro-Zionist leanings. Preston Manning has attempted to be more circumspect and judicious in his approach to the Jewish-Palestinian issue and this, in some ways, distances his attitude from Stephen Harper and the Conservative Party.

The fact that there is an interest in religion and politics by those in Canada about Christian Zionism (McDonald, Greunding, Engler), there is an depth study from the perspective of political philosophy on western theorists on religion and politics (Beiner), and a turn to international relations and religion (Rowe) means interest is afoot and growing on the dialogue about politics and religion. A new season is emerging in which religion and politics is being discussed again. The one-dimensional approach of secular versus sacred (usually to the detriment of both) is a fading season.

This book will only deal with Canadian Christian Zionism, Canadian Foreign Policy, and the Palestinians. Such an approach, however, merely reflects and embodies a much larger interest in how religion can be applied, in this case, in a problematic clash of civilizations tendency; the implications of Christian Zionism (whether benign and apolitical or decidedly political) does need to be faced. The definition of what it means to be a Canadian hovers and hangs in the balance on how Canadians view Israel—will we be brokers of peace or perpetuators of the war of one tribe against another? Canadian Christian Zionism buys into the latter; the former is what it means to be moderate lovers of peace and reconciliation.

I should make it clear at the outset that the Jewish people have suffered and suffered immensely in their communal journey through time; centuries of the diaspora and the sheer evil of the Holocaust must be kept front and centre when discussing Christian Zionism and the Palestinians. Those who ignore the painful and graphic victimization that many Jews experienced will never understand the reasons for their legitimate need for security, protection, and the "Never Again" national voice. Sadly so, the Palestinians have become the victims of the victims.

Is there a way out of such a malaise and cul-de-sac? Is there a higher ethical standard that leans towards peace rather than reinforcing mutual fears and a war of all-against-all mentality? The underlying thesis of this book is that Christian

Preface

Zionism has a predictable way of reinforcing the worst forms of Jewish nationalism and perpetuating a negative view of both Christian and Muslim Palestinians.

Those who question the unhealthy alliance of Christian Zionists and Jewish nationalists do not uncritically doff their caps to the Palestinian political parties such as Hamas, Fatah, or the PLO. Edward Said, although critical of Christian and Jewish Zionism (and the American-Israeli alliance), was a vigorous critic of Arafat and other Palestinian leaders who distorted the best of the Palestinian way. Is there a way to bring together the higher and nobler ethical vision of the Jews, Christians, and Palestinians for the greater good of Israel-Palestine, the Middle East, and the global community? There are, indeed, cracks where the light can get in, but the alliance of Christian Zionism and Jewish Zionism is certainly not where the light can appear—in fact, the dove is never free in such a context.

I have asked, by way of conclusion, four friends (Brad Jersak, Andrew Klager, Wayne Northey, and Archbishop Lazar Puhalo) to reflect in Afterwords on the ideology of Christian Zionism, their more personal experiences with Christian Zionism, and why such a form of ideology inflames the clash between Jews and Palestinians rather than healing the breach.

May 2014
Fiat Lux
Ron Dart

CHAPTER 1

A TANGLED TALE

Thousands of books describe various aspects of the Palestinian-Israeli conflict. Only a handful detail Canada's ties to the dispute and most do so from a pro-Israeli perspective.[1]

Harper has backed Israel with such fervour that veteran scholars and diplomats rank it as the most dramatic shift in the history of postwar Canadian foreign policy.[2]

The treatment of the Palestinians since 1947 is a blot upon a decent world. Pushed out of their ancestral homes and harried and attacked in the dwellings which they temporarily acquired, they have been brutalized, denigrated, and, at best, ignored. Why have these people been forced into a dreary diaspora in a world in which concern for human rights is supposed to be a watchword? After seeing the tragedy of the Palestinian refugees, I was never the same again.[3]

A third observation based on the The Ipsos Reid exit poll is that the Conservatives did well among Jewish

---

[1] Engler, *Canada and Israel*, 4.

[2] McDonald, *Armageddon Factor*, 311.

[3] Macquarrie, *Red Tory Blues*, 310f.

> voters in the 2011 election but that they did poorly among Canadian Muslims. Among Jewish voters, 52 percent voted Conservative, compared to 24 percent who voted Liberal and only 16 per cent who voted NDP. The Harper government has courted Jewish voters by offering uncritical support for Israel.[4]

CANADA PLAYED A SIGNIFICANT role through the United Nations in the founding of the state of Israel in 1948. Lester Pearson (former Liberal Prime Minister of Canada and recipient of the Nobel Peace Prize in 1956) was front and centre as a Canadian in bringing the state of Israel into being. Needless to say, the Jewish, Christian, and Muslim communities (both religious and secular) have been divided on how to interact with and justify or oppose the state of Israel. There are Jewish, Christian, and Muslim hawks just as there are Jewish, Christian, and Muslim doves who are part of this larger clash of civilizations that seeks to understand how to hold together the tendency to clash with the deeper desire to peacefully co-exist.

The article by Joseph Rosen, "The Israel Taboo: Money and sex aren't the only things Canadians don't talk about" (*The Walrus*: January/February 2014), highlighted—in a thoughtful, graphic, and succinct manner—why it is difficult (in this case, for Rosen, as a Canadian Jew) to discuss Israel in a minimally critical manner; polarization and name baiting often dominates the day. Rosen placed the Canadian Jewish situation in a not-to-be-forgotten context and setting:

---

[4] Gruending, *Pulpit and Politics*, 2.

CHAPTER 1 – A TANGLED TALE

Canadian Jews, while liberal in many ways, are surprisingly right wing when it comes to Zionism. According to a census analysis done in 2006, 25 percent of American Jews identify as Zionist, while 42 percent of Canadian Jews do. Toronto and Montreal have some of the highest rates of visitation to Israel of any Jewish community in North America, at 75 percent. This gives the impression of a seemingly univocal, unconditional support for the Israeli state in Canada, at least within the Jewish community.[5]

The fact that Canada played a key role in the founding of the state of Israel, and "[a]fter World War II, Montreal received the third-largest group of Holocaust survivors in the world,"[6] means that there is a tale to be told about Canada and Zionism that has not yet been expressed. There is, of course, the Christian Zionist tale that antedates Jewish Zionism, as well as the Jewish narrative and the Palestinian story. There are all sorts of suggestive nuances within these groups and between them, but the complex Canadian Christian Zionist narrative is often trumped by the history of Christian Zionism from other countries.

Those who study the origins, development and contemporary expressions of Christian Zionism often track in two directions. There are those who highlight, within Christian history, the anti-Semitic and "Teaching of Contempt" tendencies that have dogged Christianity and Christendom. Then, there are those who track and trace the philo-Semitic, "Teach-

---

[5] Rosen, "The Israel Taboo," http://thewalrus.ca/the-israel-taboo/.
[6] Ibid.

ing of Esteem," and Christian Zionist commitments in England, Germany, and the United States. The fact that Canada is often left out of this discussion does need to be noted. Canada has, to some degree, been shaped and influenced by both the British and American connections, and the Christian Zionist tendencies from these states have done much to determine the present Christian Zionist position in the ruling political party in Canada today. This essay will touch on both historic Christian Zionism in Canada and the disturbing reality of Christian Zionism at the highest levels of political power and foreign policy decision-making in Canada today by the majority government of Conservative Prime Minister, Stephen Harper.

The United Nations General Assembly voted on 29 November 2012 with a margin of 138 to 9 to recognize Palestine as a non-member observer state. This vote opened the door for Palestinian statehood. It is significant to note that of the nine states that opposed the resolution, Canada and the United States were the most prominent. In fact, the Foreign Affairs Minister of Canada, John Baird, suggested that Canada might even take retaliatory measures against the Palestinians for forcing the statehood agenda onto the global stage. The United Nations General Assembly has proclaimed that 2014 will be the International Year of Solidarity with the Palestinian People. The United States, Canada, Australia, Israel, Marshall Islands, Micronesia and Palau were the only seven states to cast negative votes to oppose this initiative. Rosen's observation again on Canada and Zionism is worth heeding: "It is hard to conceive of Jews as an oppressed minority when our prime minister fully supports Israel, has established the Canadian Parliamentary Coalition to Combat Antisemitism, and works overtime to court the Jewish vote."[7]

Why has the ruling Conservative Party in Canada taken such a pro-Zionist perspective, does Canada have a history of taking such a position, and what might be some of the reasons for Canadian Christian Zionism? This book will answer some of these questions in a suggestive way.

---

[7] Ibid.

CHAPTER 2

DAWN OF THE DILEMMA

The moral truth in the Middle East is not the monopoly of either Israel or the Arab states. Nor is it simply at some midpoint between them. The terrible truths in that conflict are trapped in a labyrinth—a bitter zigzag maze of grievances and wrongs on all sides. One cannot find these truths in aloofness but only in the zigging and zagging through the tangles of history and in fellowship with living men and women of the nations and religions involved. Indignation is the least helpful moral stance in the Middle East. Sorrow is much more appropriate—not a passive sorrow but an active sorrow that never forsakes the works of reconciliation and reconstruction.[8]

THE DAWN OF CHRISTIAN ZIONISM in Canada can be tracked to the significant presence of Henry Wentworth Monk in the 19th century. Monk had both decidedly philo-Semitic tendencies and he attempted to translate such leanings into the purchase of land for the Jews in Palestine. Monk was aggressively active in the 1870s–80s in the effort in buy land

---

[8] Geyer, "Introduction," In *Peace, Justice*.

CHAPTER 2 – DAWN OF THE DILEMMA

for God's chosen people. Monk was initially introduced to such notions by the Earl of Shaftesbury (Anthony Ashley Cooper) in about 1840. The Earl of Shaftesbury was the leading Christian Zionist in England in the latter half of the 19th century, and Shaftesbury (as a leading English evangelical Zionist) did much to influence Arthur Balfour and the Balfour Declaration of 1917. Monk called for a "Dominion of Israel," and he even wrote a letter to Balfour in 1896 entitled "Stand Up O Jerusalem." Monk's philo-Semitic commitments were amply spelled out in *For the Time is at Hand: An Account of the Prophecies of Henry Wentworth Monk of Ottawa, Friend of the Jews* (Richard Lambert, 1947). Monk was a visionary of sorts, a mulligan mix of Blake, Tolstoy, and Whitman. He laboured long and hard for both world peace and the establishment of peace for Jews in their homeland; when he died in 1896, he was remembered with much fondness by many. In fact, Holman Hunt's painting of Monk hangs in the National Gallery in Ottawa.

Monk was definitely not alone in his commitment to the Jewish people and passion for the return of the Jews to their historic homeland, although, in some ways, he was distinctly ahead of his time on a variety of issues. The 19th century was a bubbling cauldron of biblical prophecies and their interpretation and application to the Jews and their promised land. Like Monk, the Reverend Albert Thompson stood within such a line and lineage. Thompson argued strenuously that Christians, in supporting the return of the Jews to their ancestral homeland, were facilitating the second return of Christ. Thompson was active, as a Canadian, in the late 19th and early 20th centuries in linking prophetic texts from the Bible to current events and their biblical meaning.

It would be impossible to ignore, in such an overview, the significant work of the Revered William Lovell Hull. Hull was from Winnipeg and was, as a missionary, "connected with *Eretz Israel* (Land of Israel) and its people since 1935." Hull was so taken by both the way the Jews were a fulfillment of prophecy and the way they made the desert bloom that most of his life's work was committed to getting the message out that Canadians (and others) should support the growing influence of the Jews in Palestine. The summa of Hull's life work was published in 1954 as *The Fall and Rise of Israel: The Story of the Jewish People During the time of their Dispersal and Regathering*. The tome is an apologetic *tour de force* to Christians (and others who cared to listen) for support of the return of the Jews to Israel. The book is packed with a historic overview of the Jews in their diaspora and their regathering to the land promised to them in prophecies. Hull's book became a sensation of sorts for many Christians on the pro-Zionist trail, and a recognized Christian publishing company—Zondervan—was willing to publish it. Hull's "Preface" speaks volumes about both his audience and agenda: "This book, though I hope that it will find favour with both Jewish and Gentile readers of all faiths, is primarily written for evangelical Christians who are interested in the fulfillment of prophecy which has been so evidently revealed in the present return of Israel to its land after nineteen hundred years of exile. . . . This book is an answer to many friends throughout the United States, Canada and the United Kingdom, who have asked me to put in print that which I have

CHAPTER 2 – DAWN OF THE DILEMMA

so frequently spoken about in many meetings."[9] Hull also remarks,

> If my writing serves to soften Gentile feelings towards Israel and the Jewish people; if it brings an understanding to both Christians and Jews of the hand of God in preserving and restoring Israel; if it enables the reader to realize in at least a measure the spirit which has possessed the *halutzim* (pioneers) and the army and people of Israel in repossessing and defending their land, I shall feel that I have succeeded in my purpose.[10]

It is apt to note that *The Fall and Rise of Israel* was published in 1954, and it was in 1953 that the Soviet Union broke off diplomatic ties with Israel. In his book, Hull includes an abridged speech by David Ben Gurion (Israel's first Prime Minister) defending the Jewish people and the state of Israel against the position taken by the USSR. The decision by the Soviet Union to break off ties with Israel in 1953 further clarified, in the Cold War, who were going to be the friends of Israel and who the enemies.

The import of Hull's preface to note are fourfold, and these points, in many ways, did much to shape and define significant aspects of the evangelical attitude towards Israel in Canada in the 20th century. First, Israel is God's chosen people, and to support the Jews and the birth of Israel is part of the fulfillment of biblical prophecy. Second, Hull played a significant role in the evangelical ethos in the United States, Canada, and the United Kingdom on the lecture circuit in

---

[9] Ibid., 9f.

[10] Ibid., 10.

affirming the chosen People–chosen Land–prophecy synthesis. Third, Hull had lived in Palestine from 1935, so he spoke with a certain authority on the issue. Fourth, and not least in importance, it was Hull's conversation with Justice of the Supreme Court of Canada, Ivan Rand, when he was in Palestine in June/July 1947 with the United Nations Special Committee on Palestine (UNSCOP) that was a game-changer for Rand on the position he would finally take on the Palestinian question.

Hull created in 1936 the Zion Apostolic Mission that he directed until 1961. It has since then become the Jerusalem Cornerstone Foundation in which the Kopp family tradition has carried on the Hull vision. During his years in Palestine, Hull also published a pro-Zionist paper entitled "Christian Voice in Israel." There are certain compromises that must be made for those who see themselves as missionaries to the Jews—Palestinians are often sacrificed on the altar to appease the demands of the Jewish State and its security interests. Hull was a prominent and significant Canadian in such a worrisome process.

The short lecture by Yanky Fachler in Dublin entitled, "Christian clergymen who changed the course of Zionist history" (July 2011), listed Rev. William Blackstone, Rev. William Hechler, Rev. John Stanley Grauel, and—to the point of this essay—the Rev. William Lovell Hull as the four main Christian clergymen who ushered in the Christian Zionist vision; Hull was the only Canadian in the Zionist hall of heroes.

It should be noted before parting paths with Hull that he was the minister, spiritual advisor, and confessor of sorts to Adolf Eichmann, and in his timely book, *The Struggle for a*

CHAPTER 2 – DAWN OF THE DILEMMA

Soul (1963), he lists the content of his thirteen visits to Eichmann and the three letters he received from Eichmann. The book concluded with reflections on "The Execution" and "Ashes to Ashes-Dust to Dust." At the time, Hull seemed to be the pre-eminent Canadian Christian Zionist, but his deeper Pentecostal fundamentalism became more apparent both in the book and later interviews. Hull suggested that if Eichmann confessed his sins and accepted Christ as his personal saviour, his multiple crimes would be forgiven. He went even further, however, when he told a Toronto newspaper correspondent that the six million Jews who perished in the Holocaust were doomed to Hell because they had not accepted Christ. He also suggested that "Eichmann's sins were not as great as those of the average man who denied Jesus as the redeemer."[11] Needless to say, such statements could not help but infuriate the Jewish population of Israel and beyond. The more public and obvious crudeness of Hull's position might explain why he left Israel in 1963.

Let me all too briefly mention the crossroads dinner between Hull and Ivan Rand. Hull's commitments as a Canadian did much to shift Rand's views of the Jewish-Arab tensions and conflicts through the use of reading biblical history. Ivan Rand (who will be discussed shortly) was appointed by Louis St. Laurent to be the Canadian representative on UNSCOP. This was a divided committee, but when Rand was in Palestine in 1947, he had a lingering dinner with Hull. Here, Hull explained in meticulous detail why the Jews should have their homeland and that to ignore such a pressing need would wreak havoc for the future. Rand was

---

[11] Malachy, *American Fundamentalism*, 103–105.

duly impressed by his dinner with Hull, and many credit the Hull-Rand dinner with swaying Rand in a more Jewish direction. It is essential to note that Rand wrote a glowing and pithy foreword to *The Fall and Rise of Israel*. Rand had this to say about his dinner with Hull in the foreword: "Mr. Hull knew nothing of this effect of that luncheon talk until this foreword had been pursued by him, but I feel confident that he will count that day as not having been without its fitting deed."[12]

Canada had a tendency until UNSCOP was established to favour the British position on Palestine, which, imperfectly so, attempted to walk a middle path between the demands of both Jews and Arabs. Such a position was unworkable by 1947, as the violence in Palestine and Jewish refugees coming in on ships (like the historic Exodus event) was mounting. President Truman tended to take a more pro-Jewish position in regards to Palestine, and Britain and the United States were butting horns on the issue. It was Ivan Rand who "turned the scales" in UNSCOP in the direction of partition.

The leading Canadian expert on the Middle East at the time was Elizabeth MacCallum. Her position was that two mutually exclusive nationalisms were at the core of the problem, intensified by the Palestinian Arabs' struggle to find their way after centuries of Ottoman Turkish rule and the Jewish experience of the diaspora and the obvious raw reality of the Holocaust. Rand certainly took the time to hear and heed MacCallum, but Hull's impact and the biblical prophetic tradition proved more decisive. It can certainly be legitimately

---

[12] Ivan Rand, "Foreword," in Hull, *Rise and Fall*, 7.

argued that Hull more than most Canadians tipped the balance in favour of the Jews via Rand and, latterly, Pearson.

David Bercuson, whom I will discuss later, had this to say about Rand's UNSCOP visit to Palestine in June 1947 in his ground-breaking book, *Canada and the Birth of Israel: A Study in Canadian Foreign Policy* (1985):

> The time Rand, and other community members, spent with Horowitz, Eban, and men like Hull was important in moulding their thinking about the Palestine question because pro-Zionist positions were presented in an intimate atmosphere and at an informal and personal level. These views were not balanced by any similar contact with Palestine Arabs because of the boycott imposed by the Arab Higher Committee. . . . Rand did not become an instant and intense partisan of the Zionist cause as a result of these experiences, and continued to maintain his judicial impartiality in both public and private sessions of the committee, but it is clear that his touring helped form three basic conclusions that marked his contribution to UNSCOP's final report: the mandate must end as soon as possible; the Jews must have a state of their own in Palestine; partition was the only hope for a solution to the Arab-Jewish conflict in Palestine.[13]

The biblical tendencies—and to a lesser degree the prophetic elements—that dominated much of the 19th and 20th centuries in England, Germany, and the United States had an impact at

---

[13] Bercuson, *Birth of Israel*, 86.

the highest levels in Canada. As already mentioned, Rand and Pearson played significant roles on UNSCOP, but his biographer, William Kaplan, wisely describes and recounts other events in Rand's complex and controversial life in his book, *Canadian Maverick: The Life and Times of Ivan C. Rand* (2009), including Rand's legal journey to the Supreme Court and many of the tough decisions he made in his life. In particular, Kaplan highlights Rand's work with UNSCOP and the long-term impact of Hull on Rand in "Chapter 6: Rand Tackles the Palestine Problem." Having supported Israel and the Hebrew University—which includes the Ivan Rand Chair of Law—until his death in 1969, Rand has become an icon in Israel, and in 1954 a forest was planted in Israel in his honour. It is somewhat intriguing the way Kaplan, in a brisk and swashbuckling paragraph, turns on Martin Buber and Judah Magnes; there can be no doubt where Kaplan's prejudices dominate. I am not sure Rand would have dismissed Buber and Magnes (who taught at the Hebrew University) in such a curt and reactive manner. We can still see, therefore, the Jewish Zionist tendencies in a biographer that goes beyond even the position of Rand.

The roles of Monk, Thompson, Hull and Rand have been briefly touched on in this overview of Canadian Zionist tendencies, but Lester Pearson is very much the main actor on the stage. Pearson was raised in a home in which the Bible was the main book that one and all should know and internalize. Pearson often mentioned that when he was a young boy in Sunday School, he learned more about the towns from Dan to Beersheba than Victoria to Halifax. The fact that the Bible was a foundation document to Pearson's generation (and those before him), and the Jews are the preeminent

CHAPTER 2 – DAWN OF THE DILEMMA

players in the Bible, means that a certain DNA was placed in the soul, mind, and imagination of those in Canada about the Jews and their Promised Land; the Holocaust merely triggered a religious reflect action. Pearson is a peacemaking icon of sorts in Canada for his work on the Suez Crises, and he won the Nobel Prize in 1956 for such efforts. But there is much more to Pearson than this shining Knight image. Pearson had decidedly Zionist leanings, and he often made it clear that he had taken in such a position from his Christian upbringing. Rand had been profoundly shaped and influenced by the influential American Zionist and Supreme Court Judge, Louis Brandeis. Pearson has been called the "Lord Balfour" of Canada and "Rabbi Pearson," and prominent Zionists have presented him with some of their highest awards.

Pearson did, in being fair, walk a narrow tightrope on the Jewish-Palestinian issue. The Americans by 1948 were much more Zionist than Canada. William Lyon McKenzie King leaned more in the British direction that attempted to mediate between Jews and Arabs; Pearson was caught on the horns of this dilemma, but he certainly played a key role in the partition of 1948 that set the Jews free to have their homeland. In 1960, he was recognized by the Jews for his significant diplomatic efforts when they awarded him Israel's Medallion of Valour. When Trudeau replaced Pearson as prime minister, Pearson was offered the Theodore Herzl award from the Zionist Organization of America in 1968; Pearson's "commitment to Jewish freedom and Israel" did not go unnoticed. From 1947 to 1948, Pearson, much more than Rand, was front and center in formally bringing into existence the state of Israel. So, how would Pearson view Stephen Harper's position on Israel? I suspect, as a thoughtful

Canadian diplomat and peace monger, Pearson would take Harper to task on his simplistic and confrontational approach to the dilemma. But it should be noted that Pearson, like Rand, was a significant actor on the Canadian stage in facilitating the emergence of the state of Israel.

In this chapter, I have merely pointed to the dawn of Christian Zionism in Canada by mentioning Monk, Thompson, Hull, Rand, and Pearson. The fuller tale can be heeded and heard by reading the texts mentioned or sifting and sorting through David Bercuson's *Canada and the Birth of Israel: A Study in Canadian Foreign Policy* or Eliezer Tauber's *Personal Policy Making: Canada's Role in the Adoption of the Palestine Partition Resolution* (2002). There can be no doubt, however, that Canadians in the 19th and 20th centuries have played significant roles in shaping Canadian foreign policy in a pro-Zionist path and direction. The dawning of such a position emerged in the 19th century; the 20th century witnessed the maturing and consolidation of such a position.

CHAPTER 3

CANADIAN ACADEMICS AND CHRISTIAN ZIONISM

I MENTIONED ABOVE THAT ONE approach to being pro-Zionist from within the Christian tradition is to list, in historic detail, all the atrocities heaped on the Jewish nation by Christians. Understandably so, such an approach creates empathy for the plight and victim-hood for the Jews. The publication of William Nicholls' *Christian Antisemitism: A History of Hate* (1993) makes it abundantly clear that there is a distinctive Christian tradition from the beginning, through the centuries, and into the present that is anti-Semitic. Nicholls taught in the Religious Studies department at the University of British Columbia (I did my MA with him) for many a decade, and he had decidedly pro-Zionist leanings. Those who take the time to heed Nicholls' detailed arguments cannot but be held by the fact that Christians have been powerful oppressors, and the Jews have again and again been hapless victims. The natural human reaction to such a reading of Christian-Jewish history is to bend the knee to the needs and demands of the Jewish people. Who, in their right mind, wishes to participate in the oppression and victimization of another people? *Christian Antisemitism: A History of Hate* has played a significant role in Canada, in both the Christian and Jewish communities, in garnering support for the state of Israel.

There is more, though, to *Christian Antisemitism* than a detailed historic listing of the treatment of Jews by Christians and secular states. Nicholls was also interested in the revisionist read of St. Paul and Jesus in post-WWII Biblical Studies. Did St. Paul and Jesus turn against their Jewish heritage? Did St. Paul elevate grace and demean the law in the way many think? Should the Jewish story and Judaism still remain a central feature of Christian thought or has such a religious way been replaced and superceded? There was a significant approach to the Bible by Christian scholars after WWII that was much more inclined to read the New Testament in a more favourable and irenical way; such was the equally important part of Nicholls' *Christian Antisemitism*.

The publication of Don Lewis' *The Origins of Christian Zionism: Lord Shaftesbury and Evangelical Support for a Jewish Homeland* (2010) seems, on the one hand, to be opposing the thesis of Nicholls. Lewis makes it abundantly clear in his tome that British evangelicals and German Pietists played a significant role in the foundation of the state of Israel through their philo-Semitism and support of a Jewish homeland. In short, there is more to the Christian Tradition than an anti-Semitic history of hate. Primarily, the British evangelical tradition was decades, indeed centuries, ahead of Jewish Zionism in arguing and urging, at the highest levels of British politics, the need to create the conditions for a Jewish homeland. Both Lewis and Nicholls, for different reasons and as Canadians, have articulated arguments that can easily be used to justify both Christian and Jewish Zionism. I have highlighted in *Holy Land Studies* how both Nichols and Lewis

CHAPTER 3 – CANADIAN ACADEMICS

have pandered to the ideology of Zionism from different academic perspectives.

There is little doubt that the foremost and most in-depth work on Canada and Israel (to the birth of Israel) is David Bercuson's *Canada and the Birth of Israel: A Study in Canadian Foreign Policy* (1985). Bercuson had published an earlier book, *The Secret Army* (1983), in which, as he states succinctly and clearly in the "Preface":

> This is a history of the Arab-Israeli war of 1948—the Israeli War of Independence. It is different from other books on that war, however, because it is the story of the *mahal*—the more than 5000 foreign volunteers who served with the Israeli forces—and of Israel's efforts to obtain the modern military equipment necessary to win the war and establish itself as a newly independent country.[14]

The fact that Bercuson had definite leanings in *The Secret Army* meant that, to a greater or lesser degree, the choice of his next topic and interpretation of it would tilt in a predictable direction. There can be no doubt where Bercuson's loyalties reside in *Canada and the Birth of Israel*. Bercuson sides with the Jews and Israel, and—in a step by step manner—he points out the slow moving position of Canada at the highest levels of foreign policy on working for the birth of Israel. This does not mean that Bercuson does not offer kudos where kudos are due: the Canadian Palestinian Committee headed by a former Anglican priest (Herbert Mowatt), Hull, Rand, and Pearson are recognized as signif-

---

[14] Bercuson, *Birth of Israel*, xiii.

icant actors on the stage, whereas those who approached the issue in a more nuanced way such as Elizabeth MacCallum and, more to the point, A.E. Prince[15] and C.E. Silcox[16] are curtly dismissed as unreliable interpreters of the situation. Bercuson, to his credit, was the first to do a serious read of Canadian foreign policy in regards to Israel, but the tale that Bercuson told should also be read with some discernment. The fact that Bercuson tends to be dismissive of King because he leaned in a more British contra American position on the Palestine question does need to be recognized; King took such a position for the simple reason that he realized that the British had a complex experience in Palestine with Jews and Arabs, and he was acutely aware that the United States did not have such a history in the area. King, like Pearson, knew violence would be the order of the day (as it was) if decisions by the UN and individual states were not handled in a judicious manner. Bercuson's book is still a must read, though, for the week-by-week involvement of Canada and the founding of the state of Israel.

There is no doubt that Lewis and Nicholls have had a limited readership, and Bercuson has moved the discussion about the birthing of Israel far from the theological and political wrangling in England and the United States. Bercuson, to give him his due, grounds his study within the Canadian context. Bercusion taught at the University of Calgary most of his days, and, to some degree, his right of centre military leanings give him some affinities with another Canadian Zionist.

---

[15] Prince, "Problem of Palestine."

[16] Silcox, "Impasse," 128–132.

Paul Charles Merkley (professor emeritus of History at Carleton University in Ottawa), in many ways, complements Bercuson. Merkley is a Lutheran, stands within the Christian Zionist tradition, and is supportive of the International Christian Embassy Jerusalem, founded in 1980 as a Christian presence to support Israel and Jerusalem as its capital. There can be no doubt that Merkley stands within a historic form of German philo-Semitism / Christian Zionism that Lewis articulated so well in *The Origins of Christian Zionism* (2010). There is a historic form of Lutheran-Anglican Zionism that is often ignored but that Merkley (and others, including the Anglican Christ Church in Jerusalem) embodies. Needless to say, many Anglicans and Lutherans do not take such a position. The article, "Christian Zionism," by Diana Swift in the online version of the *Anglican Journal* (April 17, 2014) threads together various responses to the Zionist challenge, including comments by Merkley.[17]

The publication of Merkley's *The Politics of Christian Zionism: 1891–1948, American Presidents, Religion and Israel: The Heirs of Cyrus* (1998) and *Christian Attitudes towards the State of Israel* (2001) have consolidated and clarified, for the interested and committed, the historic debate within the Christian community in a probing and controversial manner. Merkley has rarely flinched from using his skills for the pro-Zionist cause, and his many Canadian backers have more than applauded his interpretive read of the Jewish-Christian approach to the state of Israel. The fact that Merkley taught in Ottawa (the seat and centre of political power), and the equally significant fact that he was publishing on these

---

[17] Swift, "Christian Zionism," http://www.anglicanjournal.com/articles/christian-zionism.

issues as the right of centre political agenda was coming to power in Canada, meant that he became the definite and definitive academic authority for the up-and-coming political leadership in Canada. Merkley, much more than Lewis and Nicholls, has done much to shape and clarify the Zionist position for the leadership in the ruling Conservative Party in Canada. In fact, Merkley became a key advisor to Stockwell Day on Canadian-Jewish-Zionist relations when Day was head of the Alliance Party (forerunner of Harper's Conservative Party of Canada). In fact, Day and James Lunney (Conservative MP) chaired the Israel Allies Caucus that was created in 2009. The Israel Allies Caucus is a child of the Knesset's Christian Allies Caucus. The goal of the Christian Allies Caucus is to create support for Judeo-Christian values (which, when decoded, means Jewish-Christian Zionism) at high levels of politics. When Harper defeated Day for leadership of the Party, Day was offered a leadership role in the newly formed Conservative Party on significant foreign policy issues. The Merkley-Day-Harper-Zionist agenda knit together the academic and formal party politics that significantly altered the traditional attitude of Canada to the Jews and Israel.

CHAPTER 4

BIBLICAL EXEGESIS AND CHRISTIAN ZIONISM

IT SHOULD BE NOTED THAT THERE has been, since WWII and the Holocaust, a re-read and reinterpretation of Paul and Jesus' relationship to Judaism. This revisionist read was led by Paul Van Buren, Krister Stendahl and E.P. Sanders, but on the West Coast of Canada, Lloyd Gaston (who taught at Vancouver School of Theology for many years) took the definitive lead. The close collaboration between William Nichols (whom I mentioned above) and Gaston is essential to understanding how the mainstream church has—in a post-Holocaust ethos—reread Paul and Jesus in a way in which Christianity and the Church have not supplanted, replaced, or superseded Judaism. In *Paul and the Torah* (1987), Gaston spelled out in detailed arguments this more nuanced and sophisticated read of Paul and the Law. Needless to say, scholars like Van Buren, Stendahl, Sanders, and Gaston approach their support of the Jews, Judaism, and the state of Israel from a different place and for different reasons than the more populist exegetical tradition that has been committed to the Zionist agenda and cause. It is this mainstream church tradition, as also found in Niebuhr, Tillich, and many others, that has reshaped the Protestant view of the Jews and Israel.

Pope John XXIII wrote a touching and tender penitential prayer before his death on June 3, 1963. The prayer speaks volumes about the Roman Catholic change of direction after WWII and the Holocaust:

> We now acknowledge that for many, many centuries blindness has covered our eyes, so that we no longer see the beauty of Thy chosen people and no longer recognize in its face the features of our first-born brother. We acknowledge that the mark of Cain is upon our brow. For centuries Abel lay low in blood and tears because we forgot Thy love. Forgive us the curse that we wrongfully pronounced upon the name of the Jews. Forgive us that we crucified Thee in the flesh for the second time. For we knew not what we did . . .

We can also see how the Roman Catholic Church has taken a decidedly irenical view of the Jews, Judaism, and the state of Israel since Vatican II. Much of this has to do with different reads and interpretations of Paul and Jesus and their relationship to the Judaism of their time (and what this means for post-Holocaust Jewish-Christian inter-faith dialogue for our ethos). Certainly, the life and writings of Pope Benedict XVI and Scott Hahn within the Roman Catholic Church have deepened the pro-Jewish sentiments and furthered the commitments of Vatican II to Jews, Judaism, and Israel (although the latter is always problematic in inter-faith dialogue). Those who linger too long at the safer site of inter-faith dialogue (in this case Jewish-Christian) but never touch down on the tougher political realities of justice and peace in the Middle east (between Jews and Palestinians) are not truly doing inter-faith dialogue in a more demanding, responsible, and mature manner—sadly so, Jewish-Christian dialogue within the Roman Catholic Church (and many forms of Protestant

Christianity) often sidestep the more difficult political issues, and Palestinians are sacrificed on the altar of inter-faith dialogue.

The complex and often contradictory nature of Christian responses to the Jews, Judaism, and Israel at an exegetical and theological level have also unfolded at a multiplicity of organizational levels. I mentioned above P.C. Merkley— *Christian Attitudes toward the State of Israel* is probably the best book out on the topic (although leaning in a Zionist direction). Merkley has listed, for the interested, the broad range of Christian attitudes and actions in regards to Israel that is a must-read for those who are keen to tune in to the full story since WWII and the Holocaust.

The more sophisticated approach to Judaism found in the careful exegesis and theological traditions of the Roman Catholic Church and various forms of Protestantism also has a more populist counterpart that antedates WWII by more than a century. The impact of J.N. Darby, the Scofield Reference Bible, Dispensationalism, biblical prophecy, End Times scenarios, and Zionism have been widely discussed and analyzed by many. But what role has Canada played in this linking together of biblical exegesis and Christian Zionism? Darby travelled to North America seven times between 1862 and 1877, and he spent time in Toronto, Montreal, and Ottawa. The annual Niagara Bible Conferences that were held from 1875 to 1897 moved Darby's agenda forward and inspired the young C.I. Scofield. The shift in the United States within the conservative evangelical community to the Scofield Reference Bible (first published in 1909), Dispensationalism, pre-millennialism, and a more pro-Jewish agenda did not go unnoticed in Canada.

The Plymouth Brethren tradition that Darby played a role in founding exerted a much broader influence on the conservative evangelical ethos than merely the Brethren. The publication of the Scofield Bible spread the Darbyite heritage throughout many denominations. The emphases that emerged from such a way of reading the Bible amidst many other exegetical tendencies was the centrality of the Jews, their prophetic return to the Holy Land, and an End Times scenario. This particular dispensational interpretation was not shared by all the Plymouth Brethren. The F.F. Bruce school of the Brethren was much more scholarly and opposed the Darby tradition, but the Darby-Scofield read of the Bible won the day amongst many conservative evangelicals.

I mention this important fragment within the Brethren between the more populist Darbyites and the more scholarly Bruce types for the simple reason that Regent College (which was founded in 1969 in Vancouver, British Columbia by Plymouth Brethren) was more moderate and indebted to the heritage of F.F. Bruce. This means that when Hal Lindsey (a faithful follower of Darby-Scofield with an updated apocalyptic view) was strutting his prophetic Armageddon agenda in the 1970s, Regent College opposed such a misread of the prophetic and the bestselling books by Lindsey and his acolytes. The publication of *Dreams, Visions & Oracles: The Layman's Guide to Biblical Prophecy* in 1977 by Carl Armerding and Ward Gasque (two founding professors of Regent College) made it brilliantly clear that the meaning of the prophetic should not be equated with End Times speculation and questionable historic events and people. Regent College established itself as a leading Reformed and evangelical graduate school in the 1970s–80s that, unlike many conservative evangelical Bible schools in Canada, did not follow the Darby-Scofield-Lindsey exegetical tradition with its obvious Zionist commitments.

The province of Alberta in Canada became a portal into the emerging Niagara Conferences-Darby-Scofield synthesis. William Aberhart was quite taken by the End Times dispensational scenario of Darby-Scofield and tribe, and he started the Calgary Prophetic Bible Institute (modelled somewhat on the Moody Bible Institute in Chicago). The merging of the language of prophetic with a Pro-Jewish stance (the Jews being God's chosen people) consolidated an emerging vision in Canada by the conservative evangelicals. The seeds that Aberhart had planted took root and produced a long term harvest. It did not take long for "Bible Bill's" Calgary Prophetic Bible Institute to morph into Canada's National Back to the Bible Hour (begun in 1925). Bible Bill's "Prophecy Wall Chart" that highlighted how the Bible was to be interpreted has become an iconic legend of sorts: 16.7 ft. long and 4.5 ft. high, the message could not be missed. The Back to the Bible Hour turn meant—when decoded at a political level—a defense of liberal democracy, American imperialism, anti-Communism, and philo-Semitism. Aberhart died in 1943, Ernest Manning followed lockstep in Aberhart's footsteps (becoming Premier of Alberta and guiding the Back to the Bible Hour). Ernest Manning directed the National Bible Hour from 1943 to 1989, and in 1982 he was awarded the Humanitarian Award by B'nai Brith; obviously, trips to Israel and support of the Jewish agenda through a certain read of the Bible won the day for the Jewish leadership in Canada. The Back to the Bible Hour heritage and tradition is now housed and delivered by Global Outreach Mission from St.

Catharines in Ontario. The Aberhart-Manning dynasty, though, is essential to understand a significant aspect of the shift towards a Christian Zionist perspective.

The formal founding of the state of Israel in 1948 demonstrated that the prophetic clock was moving towards the appointed hour. The Aberhart-Manning twosome had played their role in both Alberta and Canada in raising the flag of prophecy and supporting the Jewish people to their historic home. More will be said about the Aberhart-Manning-Zionist connections later in the book.

When attempting to understand Christian Zionism in Canada, it would be impossible to ignore the leadership role of Merv and Merla Watson. The Watson duo and family have done more than most to call conservative evangelicals back to Jewish festivals, music, dress, and a sort of Jewish romanticized ethos. The Watsons and their followers have made many trips to Israel, and the Jewish state has warmly welcomed their uncritical support of the Zionist ideology. Merla Watson recounted much of their pro-Jewish leadership and treks to Israel (replete with exuberant photos) in *Merla's Miracle*. The role of Merv and Merla in shaping a pro-Jewish agenda in Canada at a populist level more in the trenches has been significant and strategic. The fact that Merv emerged from a Plymouth Brethren background (with their commitment to Darby and Scofield) and Merla grew up in a Pentecostal background (with a read of the Jewish prophets that pandered to a pro-Jewish outlook) is worth noting. The well-known and warmly supported populist evangelist, Benny Hinn, is a child of the Zionist commitments of Merv and Merla Watson. The Watson duo has also been intimately involved at a variety of inspirational and pied piper levels with the International Christian Embassy in Jerusalem. I initially encountered the Watsons at St. Paul's Anglican parish in Toronto in the 1960s when they were playing folk music in the catacombs. They had begun, at that time, to make a musical turn to Judaism and the Jewish people. The "Jesus People" in Toronto in the 1960s were divided on such a move by Merv and Merla Watson. The Watson family moved to Israel in 1976, and, as Merla comments in *Merla's Miracle*,

> We felt such a burden to comfort the wounded Jewish people with song! We have come to love and respect them with all our hearts! We sang for countless Israelis, rich and poor, young and old, even the Prime Minister and the President. We gave birth to the International Christian Celebration during the Feast of Tabernacles, and the International Christian Embassy in Jerusalem.[18]

There is no doubt that Merv and Merla Watson have interpreted the Bible in such a way that the Jewish and Zionist way have become their unanalyzed hermeneutic. The fact that they were there as founders of the still thriving and influential International Christian Embassy in Jerusalem speaks much about the role a Canadian Christian couple have played in paving the way for many to follow the Zionist road.

The impact and importance of J.H. Hunter must also be recognized and acknowledged in this historic overview. Hunter was a significant Canadian Christian journalist who, from 1929–1969, edited the rather controversial *Evangelical Christian* magazine. Hunter was also a popular and well read

---

[18] Watson, *Merla's Miracle*, 6.

novelist and in 1956; Zondervan Publishing Company stated that Hunter was the "author of the quarter century." The publication of Hunter's novel *Banner of Blood* in 1947 took a decidedly pro-Zionist stance in the conflicts in Palestine. *Banner of Blood* was followed by *Thine is the Kingdom* (1951) and predated by the Middle East and biblical thriller, *The Mystery of Bar Saba* (1940). The sheer impact of Hunter's right of centre thinking in his novels (and in the *Evangelical Christian*) makes him a significant figure in Cold War Christianity and those who took the Christian Zionist position. It should be noted, though, that *Banners of Blood* is not a novel that supports a violent return of the Jews to Israel. In fact, the leading actors in the novel oppose the various and varied Jewish groups (e.g., Stern gang) that use violence to reclaim the land from the Arabs—the novel begins with a quote from *Micah* 3:10: "They build up Zion with blood, and Jerusalem with iniquity." There is a definite Christian prophetic element in *Banners of Blood*, but it is softened somewhat by a more nuanced understanding of the Jewish return to Palestine in a more nonviolent and messianic approach.

There are few who have heard of J.H. Hunter these days, but it is impossible to miss the prolific End Times writings of Grant Jeffrey on the Canadian landscape. Jeffrey, in many ways, has become the Hal Lindsey of Canada. The sheer volume of his publications (and his attentive populist audience) has placed him at the forefront of a reading and application of the Bible that positions Jeffrey well to be the Canadian voice of populist prophetic Zionism for many right of centre Christians. Jeffrey, by the time of his death in 2012, had published more than 30 books in the area of biblical prophecy, eschatology, and biblical archaeology from within a predictable dispensational evangelical tradition. Jeffrey chaired Frontier Research Publications until 2012, and it is estimated that he has sold more than 7 million copies of his books, which have been translated into more than twenty-four languages. It is somewhat fascinating to note that Grant's brother, David Jeffrey, is honoured by many evangelicals, both in Canada and beyond, for his serious, scholarly, and substantive contributions to faith, literature, and Western religious thought. Grant and David Jeffrey emerged from a fundamentalist context, but Grant has remained within this ethos, and his thinking and writing have, in many ways, much in common with Merv and Merla Watson. The publication of yet another Canadian, Jake Friesen, has furthered the End Times pro-Jewish leanings: *The Seer* (2003) by Friesen is more tempered and measured than Jeffrey, but when conclusions need to be reached, the pro-Jewish and Zionist attitude prevails and dominates. In many ways, Friesen's *The Seer* embodies the right of centre charismatic Mennonite ethos in Canada that can be found often in the Mennonite Brethren. In this overview, it is, however, impossible to omit the Alliance Church minister, William Goetz. The original publications of *Apocalypse Next* (1980) and *The Economy To Come* (1983) were received with such acclaim that both books (and many other books by Goetz on biblical prophecy and the End Times) have gone into many editions—there is, obviously, an eager audience for the writings of those like Jeffrey and Goetz.

Moreover, there are close connections between Americans and Canadians on the relationship of prophecy and Israel, and the ongoing work of David Hocking cannot be missed. Hocking began his Zionist organization of Hope for Today in 1995, and it states on his website that "David has focused in his ministry upon Bible Prophecy, especially as it relates to God's plan for Israel." I live in Abbotsford, British Columbia, and Hocking's Zionist headquarters in Canada is in Abbotsford. I have watched with some fascination a variety of conservative evangelical congregations in Abbotsford and environs uncritically genuflect to Hocking; the tragic family divisions and schismatic actions that take place on the Zionist issue for those who bend the knee to Hocking's reading of the Bible are sad to see.

Hope for Today is but one of many American-Canadian Christian Zionist organizations. Founded in 1976, Bridges for Peace (BFP) has an older pedigree, while the Canadian branch of BFP was established in 1987. Many Canadian Christian Zionists with a commitment to hands-on work in Israel support BFP. It is somewhat disturbing that the focus of BFP is more about bridges of peace between Christian Zionists and Jews in Israel than building bridges of peace between Jews, Christians, and Palestinians; such is the way words are often bent and distorted to serve questionable ends.

In Canada, there is a sense in which Jeffrey, Goetz, and Hunter have, in their different ways, reflected various forms of populist and prophetic Zionism that has found greater expression in Tim LaHaye's "Left Behind" series. The front cover of *Newsweek* (May 24, 2004) stated that LaHaye and Jerry Jenkins are "The New Prophets of REVELATION" and ponders "Why Their Biblical Novels Have Sold 62 Million Copies—And Counting." The article is called, "The Pop Prophets," and the subtitle is "Faith and Fiction: Tim LaHaye and Jerry B. Jenkins are an unlikely team with a shared evangelical fervor—and America's best-selling writers." LaHaye has in many ways taken Hal Lindsay and the End Times / "left behind" industry to a newer and higher entrepreneurial level. It might be inaccurate to call LaHaye evangelical or prophetic, but there is no doubt that he is popular and appeals to a certain naïve crowd that we also see in Canadian Christian Zionism.

The coming together in March 2004 of conservative evangelicals and Jews for the "Israel You're Not Alone" event in Jerusalem combined the movers and shakers of Canadian Zionism (including Grant Jeffrey; David Mainse; Franklin Pyles, President of the Christian & Missionary Alliance; Bill Morrow, General Superintendent of the Pentecostal Assemblies of Canada; and Charles McVety, President of Canada Christian College) with leading Jews from Israel to assure the Jewish state that they are not alone.

There is, therefore, in Canada, a direct link from Darby-Scofield, through to the Niagara Bible Conferences, up to Aberhart-Manning's National Back to the Bible Hour, the Watson's International Christian Embassy in Jerusalem, Grant Jeffrey, William Goetz, the Mennonite Brethren ethos as found in Jake Friesen and the "Israel You are Not Alone" coalition of Canadian conservative evangelicals. The ripple effect has been enormous, and the political implications must be duly recognized. Those who have grown up in such an ethos will certainly vote for a political party that takes a definite position in regards to the Jews and support for the state of Israel.

Douglas Todd had an award winning article published in the *Vancouver Sun* (July 30, 2005) entitled "Enter the Evangelicals." There were many hot button issues raised in the timely article and Christian Zionism was one of them. The subtitle of the article was "U.S. Religious Right groups have a foot in Canada's political door, and they're pushing it open." Needless to say, there are serious differences between fundamentalists and evangelicals as there are subtle shifts in differences within the evangelical tribe. Douglas interviewed me for the article, and we discussed—as one of the many contentious issues—the sub-culture of Christian Zionism and the Armageddon-"end of history" ethos that dominates such thinking. There can be no doubt that many Americans and Canadians are on the same page in such a worldview, although at the present time Harper and tribe tend to be more pro-Israeli than is Obama and the American Democrats—rare are the moments when Canada, at the highest level, is right of the United States, but we dwell at such a moment. Todd's article makes it appear as if Canadians are more moderate in the areas of religion, politics, and morality than Americans, but, since 2005 when the article was published, Canada has taken a decidedly right of centre swing (quite different, I might add) from classical Canadian High/Red Tory conservatism; blue Toryism has frozen much, and dialogue within a glacier cold ideology is virtually impossible to do. This shift to the political right in Canada has meant a commitment to Christian and Jewish Zionism and a rather uncritical attitude towards the state of Israel—the Palestinians are the victims of such a one-dimensional read and understanding of the situation.

The fact that in Stephen Harper's recent trip to Israel (January 2014) a significant number of conservative evangelicals—reflecting the "who's who" of Christian Zionism in Canada—were on the trip along with a host of Jewish rabbis (with obvious Zionist leanings) does need to be noted. There is an obvious convergence of interest between both Christian and Jewish Zionist on the state of Israel issue. Many of the leading conservative evangelical denominations, think tanks, and activist organizations such as Christian and Missionary Alliance, Pentecostal Assemblies of Canada, Fellowship of Evangelical Baptist Churches in Canada, International Christian Embassy Jerusalem-Canada, Evangelical Fellowship of Canada, and Crossroads Christian Communications television network joined Harper for his trip to Israel, as did, of course, the pro-Zionist, Stockwell Day (who is also a former Pentecostal minister).

It should be noted by way of threading to an end this section that there have been thoughtful and substantive Canadian theologians and exegetes that have thought through these issues but have come to different and more moderate conclusions. I did mention above the mild opposition to the Zionist perspective from such Canadians as Elizabeth MacCallum, A.E. Prince and C.E. Silcox. The publication in 1979 of *Peace, Justice and Reconciliation in the Arab-Israeli Conflict: A Christian Perspective* by such Canadian worthies as Cranford Pratt, Gregory Baum, John Burbidge, William Dunphy, Thomas Langan, Willard Oxtoby, and Cyril Powles (with a fine Introductory Note by Alan Geyer) holds high a tension that cannot be easily resolved by tipping the exegetical, historic, or theological hat to either one side or the other. The quest, in this challenging missive, is to discern how both peace and justice can be reconciled—rare are such booklets in the Zionist agenda. Willard Oxtoby also published a fine-tuned article on the issue that clearly pointed the way to a more nuanced read of the situation: "The Middle East: From

Polemic to Accommodation" (*The Christian Century:* October 13, 1971) that insightfully anticipated the book of 1979, just as William Dunphy, much earlier and from a different perspective, had contributed to *Benedictine and Moor: A Christian Adventure in Moslem Morocco* (1960). Needless to say, there are Canadian academics and activists who realize that the situation in Israel-Palestine is more complex than the one-dimensional Christian Zionists read it.

CHAPTER 5

THE CONSERVATIVE PARTY AND CHRISTIAN ZIONISM

IDEAS OFTEN DO, IN TIME, HAVE consequence, and this is certainly true in Canada. In his PhD turned book, *Canadian Evangelicalism in the Twentieth Century: An Introduction to Its Character*, John Stackhouse suggested that there were 'The Eccentrics' and 'The Mainstream' evangelicals in Canada. Stackhouse suggested that T.T. Shields and William Aberhart embodied much more the eccentrics.

I mentioned above that Aberhart was the founder of the Calgary Prophetic Bible Institute, host of Canada's National Back to the Bible Hour, and Premier of the province of Alberta. Ernest Manning replaced Aberhart in his dual role as Premier and radio preacher after Aberhart's death. Ernest Manning's son, Preston Manning, was the founder of a right of centre party (Reform and Alliance parties) that became the present Conservative Party of Canada now in power with a majority in Parliament.

Preston Manning was replaced by Stockwell Day (who was an staunch Zionist), and Stephen Harper replaced Day as leader of the newly formed Conservative Party of Canada. Many of Harper's Members of Parliament come from conservative evangelical backgrounds, and, as such, the pro-Jewish ethos has been bred in them by a rather questionable read and interpretation of the Jewish prophetic tradition and a

Sunday School understanding of the Jews as God's chosen people. As Marci McDonald observed in her important book, *The Armageddon Factor*, "Harper has backed Israel with such fervour that veteran scholars and diplomats rank it as the most dramatic shift in the history of postwar Canadian foreign policy."[19]

What have been some of the pro-Zionist positions that the Harper government has taken and why have they taken such positions? When Hamas was legitimately elected in 2006 to represent the Palestinian people, Harper cut aid to the Palestinians. Harper sided with the Jewish state against Lebanon in the 2006 war, and when Israel invaded Gaza in 2009 and the United Nations Human Rights Council opposed such an action, Harper stood uncritically by Israel's side. Harper opposed the decision by Hugo Chavez to oust the Israeli ambassador as a result of Israel's invasion of Gaza. Harper went so far as to suggest that he might even represent Israel in Venezuela. Harper also opposed Obama at the G8 Summit in France, in which Obama suggested a return to the pre-1967 borders. The fact must also be duly noted that the former Minister of Citizenship, Immigration and Multiculturalism, Jason Kenny, attempted to prevent George Galloway (former British MP who has sympathy with Hamas) from entering Canada. There is no doubt that Harper is much further right than the United States these days on the Zionist issue (a rather rare and unusual position for most Canadians).

There is much more that could be said about the Conservative Party in Canada and their ideological pro-Zionist stance. The Conservative Party's opposition to the

---

[19] McDonald, *Armageddon Factor*, 311.

CHAPTER 5 – THE CONSERVATIVE PARTY

Canadian International Centre for Human Rights and Democratic Development for funding "terrorist" groups in the Middle East (decoded, means anything that questions Zionism) has meant that any questioning of Zionist and settler activities in Israel is deemed terrorism. KAIROS (an ecumenical church group) also had funding cut off because it dared to question Zionist policies, and Mada al-Carmel (who was studying the treatment of women in Arab-Israel) also had support terminated. Each of the groups mentioned above had some sympathies for the plight of the Palestinians, and the Zionist-oriented Conservative Party of Canada punished such groups for daring to think and act outside the Zionist ideological stance.

The work done decades ago at a more exegetical and Bible School level by Darby, Scofield, Aberhart, Manning, and their tribe has now moved into a worrisome political phase. Men and women who took in a pro-Jewish ideology as children in Sunday School are now making decisions in Canadian foreign policy as adults. The eccentrics have become the mainstream and the Canadian mainstream has been marginalized. The implication of the eccentrics in power in Canada is ominous for both Jewish-Palestinian relations and Canadian Middle Eastern foreign policy.

The fact that Marci McDonald has been one of the few in Canada that has tracked and traced the varied connections and completed the essential dot-connecting on the Harper-Zionist love fest must be noted. McDonald's chapter, 'The Armageddon Factor,' in *The Armageddon Factor: The Rise of Christian Nationalism* probes and highlights all the formal and informal web of relations in Canada that support the present pro-Zionist foreign policy of Harper's majority government. The deeper the probes into the conservative evangelical and fundamentalist ethos in Canada, the more it will become abundantly clear how and why a certain read of the Bible is significantly impacting who is chosen as Members of Parliament in Canada and how such decisions are altering historic Canadian foreign policy in the Middle East.

CHAPTER 6

POPULIST EVANGELICALS AND CHRISTIAN ZIONISM

THE NATIONAL POST (SATURDAY, August 19, 2006) carried a full-page advertisement sponsored by Christians United for Israel calling for a 'National Day of Prayer for Israel and the Peace of Jerusalem.' A short read of the advertisement makes it quite clear that the political agenda for the day is support of Zionism. Benny Hinn and John Hagee are backers of Christians United for Israel, and the Canadian version of the organization is equally Zionist. It is significant to note that on the Christians United for Israel website, another conservative evangelical organization with decidedly Zionist leanings is recommended: the Institute for Canadian Values. The connection between Canadian values and Zionism does beg some rather worrisome questions. Do Canadian values equal uncritical support for Zionism? The CEO of the Institute for Canadian Values is Joseph C. Ben-Ami, and his website makes it rather dubious yet obvious (particularly in the recommended books) that genuine Canadian values are right of centre politically as well as Zionist. Christians United for Israel and the Institute for Canadian Values point the way to Equipping Christians for the Public Square Centre. Tristan Emmanuel is the captain and presiding chief of this organization, and there is no doubt where such a tribe rest its Zionist head.

Christians United for Israel has another companion organization in Canada that has drawn the naïve and historically illiterate. Watchman for the Nations was started by Bob Birch on the West Coast. Bob Birch was well connected with Bernice Gerard, and both have played a significant role in linking the Christian charismatic and renewal movements with Zionism. Bob Birch and Bernice Gerard have a decades long history with David Mainse of 100 Huntley Street in Burlington, Ontario, and Mainse, Birch, and Gerard have made it quite clear why and how Christianity and Zionism are one. A read of Mainse's *100 Huntley Street* and Beth Carson's *Pastor Bob: A Statesman of Prayer for Canada* connects all sorts of Canadian charismatic-renewal-Zionist dots.

The recent booklet publication of Mainse's 50 years of dominating the Canadian charismatic and conservative evangelical ethos, *Crossroads Compass: Special Commemorative Edition: Celebrating 50 years of A Passion for God, A Passion for People (1962–2012)* walks the extra mile to usher the curious into the world of Canadian right of centre politics and the media. Bob Birch and Bernice Gerard died a few years, but it was Birch and Gerard on the West Coast, Mainse and 100 Huntley Street in Ontario and, earlier, Aberhart-Manning's Back to the Bible Hour that did much to massage the Zionist message at a populist level for many Canadians. Christians United for Israel, the Institute for Canadian Values, and Equipping Christians for the Public Square stand on the shoulders of Aberhart-Manning, Birch-Gerard, and Mainse-100 Huntley Street.

David Mainse has been an endorser of the pro-Jewish International Fellowship of Christians and Jews of Canada.

CHAPTER 6 – POPULIST EVANGELICALS

The International Fellowship of Christians and Jews was founded in 1983 by Yechiel Eckstein, and it tends to focus on the plight of Jews who have returned to Israel but are living in dire conditions in Jerusalem and other parts of Israel. The International Fellowship of Christians and Jews (IFCJ) appeals to conservative evangelical Christians who are committed to the notion of the Jews as God's chosen people, but see such chosen people (many elderly and some victims of the Holocaust) living in poverty and destitution in the Holy Land. Needless to say, IFCJ in Canada does not extend the same compassion to the much greater poverty and painful living conditions of Palestinians (Christian and Muslim) in Israel, the West Bank, and Gaza. But the Christian pro-Zionist way tends to have blinkers on when it comes to who is worthy of God's justice, mercy, and compassion and who should be ignored. Most of the television visual fundraising for International Fellowship of Christians and Jews of Canada focuses on graphic and tragic stories of Jews who have made their way to the land of milk and honey but find neither milk nor honey; the weekly television program IFCJ is worth the watch if for no other reason than to get a sense of a distinct Christian-Jewish ministry that is only focused on suffering Jews in Israel. Rabbi Eckstein knows how to appeal to the Christian Zionist tribe and does so in an appealing way and manner; the heartstrings are tugged and pulled by the visual stories that are connected to the biblical tale of the Jews as God's chosen people. Such Christian "Guardians of Israel" will reap their positive reward, so they are assured, if they support the International Fellowship of Christians and Jews of Canada.

There has emerged in Canada in the last decade a youth movement that has decidedly right of centre and Zionist commitments. 4MyCanada has been led by Faytene Krystow (a child of the charismatic movement), and in many ways this movement of young adults in their late teens and early twenties is the youngest and most energetic child of Birch, Gerard, Mainse, and the organizations mentioned above. 4MyCanada brings together charismatic and Christian renewal types with Harperite republican conservatism and pro-Israeli policies in the Middle East.

Faith, Hope, No Charity: An Inside Look at the Born Again Movement in Canada and the United States is an earlier version of the Christian right and Zionism in Canada. Jerry Falwell factors large in the book, as does 100 Huntley Street. Falwell and Mainse were the finest of friends; Zionism was one of the thick ropes that bound them together. The death of Falwell meant that the Zionist torch had to be passed to someone—John Hagee was waiting in the wings with his Christians United for Israel to pick up the torch as Falwell was releasing it. I deal with these points in "Canadian Republicanism and Christian Zionism," in *The Eagle and the Ox: Contemplation, the Church and Politics* (2006).

There is a direct connection in Canada between Hagee's Christians United for Israel, Charles McVety, and Canada Christian College in Toronto. McVety has been a booster and cheerleader for both Hagee and Christians United for Israel. Hagee has been more than welcomed and embraced at Canada Christian College, and many of the Jewish Zionist leaders have spoken at the College. Needless to say, there is a close rapport between Hagee, McVety, and Jewish Zionism; Frank Dimant from B'nai Brith in Canada has, like Hagee, worked closely with McVety to further the Canadian Christian-Jewish Zionist ideology. Hagee once said when at Canada Christian College, "I am so delighted that Canada's Prime Minister (Stephen Harper) immediately denounced Hamas terrorism when he became the leader of this great nation." Ezra Levant, another friend of McVety, once said, "No world leader has been as clear as Harper has been in his support for Israel's right to defend itself." There is, therefore, within Canada—and this cannot be denied or ignored—a definite collusion between Hagee's Christians United for Israel, McVety's Canada Christian College, and the Jewish Zionism of Dimant and Levant. In fact, Dimant and McVety are so ideologically close that Canada Christian College has given Dimant an honorary doctorate.

Dimant had also forced an amiable friendship with Preston Manning and Stockwell Day—populist Zionism is also political Zionism. Marci McDonald clarified much when she stated: "Years earlier B'nai Brith had honoured Ernest Manning [Preston Manning's father] for excising the anti-Semitic elements from Alberta's Social Credit Party, and Dimant sought a similar undertaking from his son at Reform."[20] "Anti-Semitic," when decoded in such a context, often means pro-Zionist. The fact that the Jewish community in Canada is about three-hundred and eighty thousand and the Canadian evangelical community is about three and a half million means that it is more than advisable that Jewish Zionists link warm and affectionate hands and arms with conservative evangelical Christian Zionists; in this way, Dimant, Levant, and Ben-Ami form a tight Jewish Zionist

---

[20] Ibid., 320.

trinity in Canada that have formed and forged close bonds with the Christian Zionists. Likewise, it would be irresponsible to ignore the work of John Tweedie and Christians for Israel. Tweedie has made many trips to Israel, and his eighth-part series, *Why Israel? What Time Is It?* is both an apologia for End Times teachings and Christian Zionism—Tweedie, like Dimant, has received an honorary doctorate from McVety and Canada Christian College.

CHAPTER 7

CONCLUSION

THERE IS MUCH MORE THAT could be said suggestive depth and detail about the origins, development, and contemporary forms of Canadian Christian Zionism. I have, all too briefly, touched on 1) the Dawn of the Canadian Zionist Dilemma; 2) Canadian Academics and Christian Zionism; 3) Biblical Exegesis and Christian Zionism; 4) The Conservative Party and Christian Zionism; and 5) Populist Evangelicals and Christian Zionism. There is, of course, in Canada a centrist and left of centre evangelical and Christian tradition that is certainly not Zionist. There has been a sloppy tendency amongst many journalists and some academics to equate evangelicalism with right of centre politics and Zionism—this is both dishonest and inaccurate. There is, though, a form of conservative evangelicalism in Canada that has decidedly Zionist tendencies. I have highlighted, in this book, some of the people and organizations that embody such a perspective and commitment. Many of the early forms of Christian Zionism antedate Jewish Zionism, but there is a definite convergence in Canada between Jewish and Christian Zionism. It is also important to note that many of the implicit Zionist ideas that were emerging in Canada in the nineteenth and twentieth centuries (not fully discussed in this book) have, in the last couple of decades, moved from backroom Bible schools, Sunday schools and Darby-Schofield reads of the Bible to the highest levels of political power and foreign policy decision-making in Canada by Stephen Harper's Conservative Party. In short, the historic hawkish eccentric fringe in Canada has now become the dominant political position. Fortunately, in time the sun sets on all political parties, but the damage carried out in the interim for both Palestinians and Jews who oppose the Zionist ideology is deadly. Sadly so, such Canadian eccentrics have seriously tarnished and damaged the image of Canada as, at her best, a peacemaker.

There are, of course, many Jews and Christians in Canada that see all too clearly the implications for both Jews and Palestinians of an uncritical stance towards Israel. It is simply intellectually irresponsible to call those who question the actions of the state of Israel as "anti-Semitic" or "Jew haters." Such a circular way of thinking numbs and negates minimal critical thinking. This was certainly not the way of the classical Jewish prophets of old who, again and again, dared to critique the Jewish people and the nations surrounding them by a higher and more humane ethical standard that had much to do justice and peacemaking. This attempt to silence critical thought can be found in many nationalist traditions: those who question the United States are often called "unpatriotic"—perhaps it is those who dare to raise critical questions about their history and living tradition that are the most patriotic. It is absurd to think, as a Canadian, that if we question our political leaders, we would be seen as not patriotic. There is something about the moderate and judicious Canadian way that welcomes such a charitable questioning of the status quo, and it is such thoughtful and creative ways of thinking that must be applied to the Christian and Jewish Zionist ideology that so besets and bedevils us these days.

The final part of this book will conclude with a variety of reflections that deal with, directly and indirectly, Canadian

Christian and Jewish Zionism and brief articles by Brad Jersak, Wayne Northey, Andrew Klager, and Archbishop Lazar Puhalo on Christian Zionism.

APPENDIX I

GEORGE GRANT AND *EXILES FROM NOWHERE: THE JEWS AND THE CANADIAN ELITE*

GRAEME NICHOLSON HAS SUGGESTED that George Grant (1918–1988) "was Canada's most significant public philosopher" and "his writing compares favourably with the popular rhetoric of Noam Chomsky and Bertrand Russell, and reflects an excellence in the public domain of Canada, which surpasses the United States and the United Kingdom in this respect."[21] I co-edited *George Grant's Theology, Philosophy, and Politics* (University of Toronto Press) and also wrote and had published *George Grant: Spiders and Bees* (2008) and *George P. Grant: Canada's lone Wolf* (2011).

The fact that Grant had such a wide ranging theological, philosophical, and political mind and imagination meant that he read deeply and reflected meaningfully on such thinkers as Arnold Toynbee, Martin Heidegger, Louis-Ferdinand Celine, Leo Strauss, and Simone Weil. The fact that Grant would dare to read and comment on serious writers and activists who asked critical questions of the Jewish tradition (Weil in a more demanding way and Strauss in a subtler manner) made him suspect to the Jewish community.

---

[21] Nicholson, "Freedom and the Good," 323.

The equally troubling fact that Grant read and commented on some of Heidegger and Celine's philosophic and literary insights (while deploring their obvious anti-Semitism) meant some within the Canadian Jewish community targeted Grant.

The publication of *Exiles from Nowhere: The Jews and the Canadian Elite* in 2008 by Alan Mendelson (a onetime colleague of Grant in the Religious Studies Department at McMaster University in Hamilton) is, for the most part, a frontal assault on George Grant, the Grant family, and those connected with the Grant family. The many distorted reads by Mendelson of Grant are troubling and worrisome, but they do reflect an even more disturbing trend. There is a tendency within some aspects of the Canadian Jewish community that refuse to welcome any critical reflection on both the Jewish tradition and contemporary Christian Zionism; those who dare to do so are branded anti-Semitic—Jew-hater is the term for Jews who raise legitimate questions about their people.

The fact that Grant was one of the most prominent Canadian public intellectuals of the latter half of the 20th century, and the equally important fact that the Grant family has been front and centre in Canadian public life in the 19th and 20th centuries, meant that Mendelson had an obvious target that could and would serve his ideological Zionism. If he could clearly argue that Grant and family were anti-Semitic, then who would dare to raise critical questions about the Jewish people, Judaism, and political Zionism? The fact that *Exiles from Nowhere: The Jews and the Canadian Elite* has a deeper and more ominous agenda (undermining of minimal questioning of the Jewish tradition) panders quite nicely to the Christian Zionists and the present pro-Zionist Conservative Party of Stephen Harper.

Mendelson also commented on Grant's encounters with significant Canadian Jewish literary types such as Leonard Cohen, Matt Cohen, and Joseph Roth (a German Jew that held Matt Cohen). The fact that Grant had his differences with Leonard Cohen (as have other literary critics), and Grant and Matt Cohen had their differences (exclusively described by Mendelson from Cohen's side) on the vexed Jewish-Christian issue meant, for Mendelson, Grant was a triumphalist and an insensitive supersessionist. The fact that Grant, like Toynbee and Weil (in a more tough questioning manner about Jewish exclusivism and Jewish violence towards the Other), dared to ask hard questions of the Jewish inheritance tends to irritate Mendelson.

Mendelson suggested that Grant's differences with Strauss and Leonard and Matt Cohen embodied and reflected a latent and implicit genteel anti-Semitism. Grant and Weil are substantively targeted for veering into anti-Semitic territory, and the fact that Grant raised legitimate questions about some of Leonard Cohen's early prose and poetry is a reason why Mendelson questions Grant. The Matt Cohen relationship with Grant remains ambiguous and complex as indicated in Cohen's *Typing: A Life in 26 Keys* (2000). I find it problematic that in the Cohen-Grant interaction, Mendelson only describes Cohen's responses to Grant rather than a balanced and fair reflection by Grant on Cohen or some Grant scholar reflecting on the Cohen-Grant tensions.

There is a sense, from the Jewish perspective, that Mendelson's conclusions are much the same as Nicholls' in *Christian Antisemitism: A History of Hate*. Mendelson's tome (400 pages) has merely applied, mostly, via the Grant family, Nicholls' historic tour de force to the Canadian context.

Needless to say, Grant and family would have a much subtler and more nuanced read of the Jewish Bible, Jewish Tradition, and contemporary Zionism than Nicholls and Mendelson.

I conclude by quoting from Robert Fulford (an icon in the Canadian publishing industry) on Mendelson's *Exiles from Nowhere*: "Mendelson's shrewd, resourceful and highly original book will unsettle many complacencies and make all of us take another hard look at the leadership class of Canada in the 20th century. What he tells us about George Grant is breathtaking."

It is rather sad that Fulford was taken in by Mendelson's distorted reading of Grant; if he had read Grant in even a minimally meaningful manner, he would have discovered how breathtaking, indeed, is Mendelson's misread of Grant (and many other Canadians) who are engaged in the Jewish question in a more sophisticated manner than Mendelson, Fulford, and other Canadian Christian Zionists.

I find it rather shallow and intellectually irresponsible that Mendelson would take the position he did in regards to Grant, but such are the tendencies of those who brook no opposition to Zionism. Gratefully so, many are the Jews who think deeper and in a more meaningful manner about the issues—Grant certainly did and it would have been wiser and more honest of Mendelson if he had met and engaged the real Grant rather than a thin caricature that has been created for the purpose of a shoot down session.

It is most worrisome, though, that in Canada none of the major political parties (Conservative, Liberal, NDP) have dared to seriously question Zionism and the state of Israel's apartheid system. Grant dared to ask some of the harder questions about the Jewish intellectual tradition, and for doing so he was labelled by Mendelson as part of the Canadian elite that had anti-Semitic leanings and tendencies—a most worrisome means of silencing the questioning of issues that need to be questioned.

APPENDIX II

MARTIN BUBER (1878-1965), ZIONISM, AND THE PROPHETIC

I REALIZE THAT MARTIN BUBER WAS not a Canadian and, in many ways, he did not directly play a role in shaping the Canadian Christian Zionist tradition. But in a deeper sense, he offers a way beyond the more simplistic notion of Zionism and the language of the prophetic, which is often employed by many Christian Zionists to justify their uncritical support for the state of Israel.

Martin Buber is a must-know thinker in the Zionist discussion for the simple reason that as a Jew he was in the thick of the internal Jewish dialogue and offered a different way of reading and applying Jewish history. Buber began a significant aspect of his Jewish journey by initially aligning himself with Theodore Herzl and the Jewish Zionist movement in the last decade of the 19th century and the first decade of the 20th century. It was just a matter of time, though, before Buber broke with Herzl's notion of political Zionism and articulated the notion of cultural Zionism. Buber was seriously concerned with the uncritical Jewish nationalism of Herzl's Zionism and the implications of it. This does not mean that Buber was against Zionism; he merely defined its meaning in a different way and manner.

Martin Buber was one of the leading German Jews who lived in Germany in the 1920s–30s. The publication of

Buber's philosophical classic, *I and Thou* (1923), catapulted Buber to prominence in both the Jewish and larger European philosophical community. *I and Thou* is a compact and dense missive, but at the heart of the book is the position that we often live with an attitude towards life in which we see the Other (God, Nature, Humans, Ourselves) as a unique and distinct 'Thou' or as an 'It' (object to be exploited and used for personal, intellectual, or political purposes).

Buber was offered a position as a professor at University of Frankfurt-am-Main in 1930, but when Hitler came to power in 1933, Buber lost his position (because he was a Jew). Buber then took a leading position in educating the Jewish community on their distinctive and unique heritage and the need to understand and live from such a committed history at a period of time in which the tradition was being attacked. The growing anti-Semitic attitude and political activism of the Nazis meant the Jews became a prime target, and Buber (as a shepherd of his people) was targeted. Buber fled to the British Mandate Territory of Palestine in 1938 and was immediately hired at the Hebrew University (which he helped found in 1925).

WWII in Germany witnessed one of the greatest horrors in Western European history with the Holocaust. Buber was in Palestine at the time, and as a German Jew he clearly understood the issues and the need of the Jews for a homeland. Buber was a biblical scholar, grounded and rooted in the Hebrew language and the history of the Jewish people (his grandfather, Solomon Buber, was a respected Jewish and biblical scholar, also). It was quite understandable why, after WWII, the Jewish people would hold high the desperate need for a homeland to defend themselves against centuries of the diaspora and the Holocaust.

There were, of course, many secular Jews who played a substantive role in the founding of the state of Israel in 1948. There were also many Christians and Jews who attempted to discern the signs of the times and make sense of the founding of the state of Israel via a way of interpreting both the Hebrew canon and the Christian Bible. Buber was, once again, well poised to engage these issues front and centre—he had begun his journey with Herzl as a political and nationalist Zionist, translated the Hebrew canon into German (correcting many of Luther's misreads of Hebrew), fled Germany, and was a leading Jewish professor and public figure in the birthing years of Israel.

The fact that Buber was both a biblical scholar and Jewish activist who had fled Germany in the late 1930s meant that he understood the Jewish predicament of victimization. This meant he was committed (as many Jews were not) to both his I-Thou religious, philosophical, and political vision of refusing to treat the Palestinians in an I-It manner. But, underlying Buber's I-Thou insights was a biblical foundation.

Many within the Jewish community in the 1920s–30s with a dovish-peacemaking commitment could not help but be drawn to the life and writings of Mahatma Gandhi. Gandhi's nonviolent activism in South Africa and India had alerted the larger world to alternate ways of doing politics and decolonization. Gandhi had published an article in *Harijan* (November 1938) in which he responded to requests about the Jews' predicament in both Germany and Jewish-Palestine. The article was, in many ways, quite insensitive to the tragic plight of the Jews. Buber was in Palestine at the time and a good friend of Judah Magnes (President of Hebrew University). Buber and Magnes responded to Gandhi with "Two Letters to Gandhi" (April 1939). The letters are more essays and worthy of many a read. Buber and Magnes, in their replies to Gandhi, made it abundantly clear that Gandhi's nonviolent resistance in South Africa and India were of an entirely different order than the plight of the Jews in Germany in the 1930s, and the Gandhian approach of peacemaking would be folly in Germany. Buber and Magnes, therefore, cannot be accused, in their notions of Zionism and the prophetic, of being naïve idealists—there was much more to them than such a derogatory label. Ivan Rand (the Canadian delegate to UNSCOP) met Magnes when in Jerusalem in 1947 and was warmly drawn to him. Magnes and Buber had, of course, quite a different notion of Zionism and the prophetic than did Hull (who had an impact on Rand); the more we heed and hear the prophetic Zionism of Jews like Buber and Magnes (then and now), the less the dove of peace will be betrayed. It is somewhat sad and sobering that Christians (in Canada and elsewhere) know so little of the Buber-Magnes peace and justice emphasis in the prophetic Zionist tradition. Perhaps such a knowledge and understanding would assist such Christian Zionists in understanding how some Jews interpret Zionism and the prophetic in much different ways than the more populist version of it.

The publication in 1948 of Buber's *Israel & the World: Essays in a Time of Crises* brought together a variety of Buber's essays on Jewish thought and life that had been published in previous decades. *Israel & the World* was divided into five sections: Jewish Religiosity, Biblical Life, Learning and Education, Israel and the World, and Nationalism and Zion. The book is a must read for those interested in a deeper read of Jewish history, life, biblical exegesis, and a worrisome read of both Jewish nationalism and Zionism. Buber made it abundantly clear, again and again, that Zionism should not be equated with nationalism and neither should Zionism be equated with an uncritical defence of the newly formed state of Israel. The prophets of the Hebrew Bible were those who placed justice and peace above an uncritical attitude to land and people.

It is important to note, therefore, how Buber is defining Zionism (unlike the way many Christian and Jewish Zionists do). Buber's mining of the Hebrew canon and his committed to the Jewish prophetic way meant that his approach to Zionism was a prophetic rather than nationalist definition of Zionism. The classical Jewish prophets place an ethical standard higher than an uncritical attitude towards people and land, and when the people did not live up to such a prophetic standard, they were forced off the land. This means that prophetic Zionism is the higher vision and nationalist Zionist its distortion (and an idol of sorts).

The publication in 1949 of Buber's *The Prophetic Faith* yet further clarified his notion of what the mother lode of the Jewish prophetic way was and why, just as his *On Zion: The History of an Idea* (1952) linked the idea of Zionism to the notion that prophetic Zionism should not be taken captive by nationalist Zionists.

There has been a tendency by Christian Zionists to use the language of the prophetic in such a way that reduces the meaning of the prophetic to end times speculation about the return of the Jews to their historic homeland. Such a simplistic interpretation of the prophetic misses entirely the ethical vision of the Hebrew prophets in which neither land nor people are an absolute that cannot be questioned or doubted. It was Martin Buber, more than most Jewish thinkers, who embodied in his life and writings a prophetic Zionism that presents a counter narrative to the Jewish and Christian Zionists who reduce the meaning of both Zionism and the prophetic to an uncritical support for the state of Israel.

It is essential, therefore, when the language of both Zionism and the prophetic is used, that we realize there is more than one way to interpret the Hebrew canon and its applicability for our time. Buber offers such an alternate read as a Jew who has certainly lived on the anvil of the historic tragedy in Germany; the founding of the state of Israel; and the situation of the Palestinians in Israel, the West Bank, Gaza, and as refugees in other states in the Middle East and elsewhere.

APPENDIX III

JESUS, THE BEATITUDES, AND THE PROPHETIC

THE BEATITUDES HAVE BEEN called the ethical Magna Carta of the Christian vision of the inner and outer journey of faith. The church has never quite known how to deal with the Beatitudes—the ideals seem too idealistic, naïve, too inappropriate for the hardball world of political realism where ignorant armies clash by day and night and power dominates the day rather than wisdom and insight. Many of the most idealistic in the life of the church have held the Beatitudes high as the true and authentic measure of the Christian faith—others see it as an ideal that needs to be balanced with the realities of life.

Those who tend to define the prophetic in terms of end times speculation often ignore the fact that Jesus made it quite clear that those who dared to live from the centre of the Beatitudes stood within the prophetic line and lineage. The Beatitudes are, in many ways, the distillation of the Jewish prophetic way, and Jesus states that those who embody, in word and deed such a way of life, will be treated as "the prophets who were before you."

The Beatitudes set before the reader an inner and outer ethical way of life that subordinates people and land to an ethical standard. Those who claim to embody the prophetic but place people and land above the elevated ethical vision of the Beatitudes distort, domesticate, and demean the meaning of the prophetic. It is significant that the Jewish people were constantly sent into exile (land being lost and people chastened) whenever the white-hot prophetic fire of the ethical was subordinated to land and Jewish nationhood. The tale of the Hebrew canon tells the same ethical story again and again: the Jews do not live up to their high calling, prophets call them to return to such an ethical vision, hearts are hardened, empires come and scatter the Jewish people.

It is obvious, therefore, that Jesus, in the Beatitudes, brought together the finest insights of the Jewish prophetic way. Those who claim to be interpreting the Bible in a prophetic manner but ignore the Beatitudes sanitize, sadly so, the prophetic way and make an idol out of people and land. This is hardly the biblical notion of the Jewish prophets, and the Beatitudes offer a corrective to such a misread and misapplication of the Jewish prophetic vision.

The Beatitudes points the way to an inner life that is clean and pure, no crooked lines, a faith life that does not court impure thoughts or a vindictive attitude, a love of enemies and praying for those who abuse others. The Beatitudes also point the way to an outer life that is passionate about seeking justice, being a peacemaker, bringing healing where conflicts and divisions dominate the day. The threading together of the inner and outer journey is the backbone of the prophetic way and there is not even a hint in the Beatitudes that nationhood and land trump such an enlightened ethical vision.

It is essential, therefore, when we think of the prophetic that the Beatitudes are kept front and centre in such a vision. Since this book is about Canadian Zionism (and their misuse and misunderstanding of the prophetic), I conclude with two Canadians who took the position that the Beatitudes were indeed the ethical Magna Carta of the Christian way. Both men are, interestingly enough, Red Tory conservatives.

Stephen Leacock had four books published after his death in 1944: *While There Is Time: The Case Against Social Catastrophe* (1945) was Leacock at his animated, incisive, and political best—a true Canadian prophet of sorts. The initial chapter in *While There is Time,* "The Gathering Crises," ponders the post-WWII situation, and faithful to his Anglican heritage and the insights of the Archbishop of Canterbury, Leacock holds high the Beatitudes as a way forward for a just and peaceful society.

George Grant has been called one of the most important public intellectuals in Canada in the latter half of the 20th century. Grant, in many ways, stood on the older Tory shoulders of Leacock. Grant did "Five Lectures on Christianity" and in his lecture on "The Gospels," he turned to the Sermon on the Mount as a "perfect account of justice or righteousness." Grant, as I mentioned in Appendix I, was severely and unfairly criticised by Alan Mendelson in his misread of Grant. Grant was no uncritical fan of a form of nationalism that subordinated ethics to people and land. The Beatitudes were held like a high flag to remind one and all where the eyes of the soul should be focused.

Leacock and Grant were Canadian prophets of an older conservative tradition. The Beatitudes and Sermon on the Mount were, for them, an ethical alpha and omega. This meant that to reduce the meaning of the prophetic to an End Times speculation chessboard game was a silly distraction. Such a distraction, though, when taken too serious and politicized (as it now is), created the twin idols of nationalism and land; such a position, by its very prioritizing of ethical goods, creates clashes of cultures and civilizations rather than a 'just' peacemaking approach to the conflicts we live with today.

APPENDIX IV

THE JEWISH PROPHETIC TRADITION:
THEN AND NOW

THERE IS NO DOUBT WITH THE CLASSICAL and biblical phase of Judaism that the Jews play a leading role on the stage. Much of history is told and interpreted within the Jewish read of it. The choosing of Abraham, Isaac, and Jacob; the tale of Joseph and Egypt; the freeing of the Jewish slaves in Egypt by Moses; and the complicated journey to the Promised Land cannot be missed in such a narrative. The first political manifesto in the West, *Deuteronomy*, is a diverse text that combines the highest moral injunctions with some of the most gruesome nationalist positions (genocide being part of the dilemma).

Much of the biblical phase of Judaism (not, of course, to be equated with the secular state of Israel) holds high the role of the prophet. The troubling presence of the prophets (oral, major, and minor) that dominates the biblical text cannot be ignored. The Jewish prophets, again and again, warned their people to live up to high moral standards. If the Jews did so, prosperity was promised. If the Jews did not heed God's calling through the prophets, punishment and various forms of exile from the land would follow. Most of the moral tale told of Judaism in the Hebrew canon is a sad but compelling one: vision offered, promise given, moral guidance denied, exile, refining, return to land, vision offered, promises given and thwarted, exile by invading empires again and again—Assyrians, Babylonians, Medes and Persians, Macedonians, Romans, and post-Masada diaspora.

It was the prophets who dared to constantly question and criticise their nation when the gap between calling/election and distortion of the meaning of election was the order of the day and decades. The prophets, of course, were often marginalized, opposed, and challenged, but they remain the leading actors in the Jewish classical canon. In short, at the heart of the biblical tradition is the prophetic notion of God, prophets, and nation. The vocation of the prophet was to call the Jewish people to a way of life that embodied the high ethical vision of God for Jews and the nations that surrounded them. The point to note here is that within the classical Jewish tradition, criticism and questioning of the Jewish people is front and centre. It is not somehow an aberration within Jewish classical thought to uncritically accept the status quo—prophetic criticism is front and centre again and again. So, when we encounter various forms of Christian Zionism or Jewish nationalism that almost demand an uncritical stance towards the state of Israel, using the language of the prophetic to do so, we are not dealing with a historic or authentic notion of Jewish propheticism. Abraham Heschel was a student of Martin Buber before he moved to the United States, and the publication of Heschel's *The Prophets* is a must read for a more classical understanding of the Jewish prophetic way. Heschel was, in many ways, a living Jewish prophet when alive.

There have been in the 20th century many Jews who have dared to question the drift and direction of the state of Israel; often, they are treated as the prophets of old—called

Jew haters or, if not Jewish, called anti-Semitic. The voices of Israel Shahak, Norton Mezvinsky, Simone Weil, Hannah Arendt, Marc Ellis, Mark Braverman and many who are now called Jewish New Historians (Benny Morris, Ilan Pappe, Norman Finkelsten, Avi Schiaim, Tom Segev, Hillel Cohen and Baruch Kimmerling) do need to be heard. There are many debates within the post-Zionist clan, but to simply ignore or dismiss them is to thin out the more complex history of post-WWII Jewish Zionism. When both Jews and Christian Zionists refuse to seriously engage the legitimate questions of the Jewish New Historians they shut down on the potential for a meaningful prophetic dialogue.

There seems to be (and this often occurs) two irreconcilable tribes on the Israel question: there is the post Holocaust "Never Again" clan that brook little or no questioning of the Jewish state and Israeli way. Many Christian Zionists (for different reasons) often bow their heads respectfully and dutifully to such a Jewish nationalist agenda. Then, there are the varied debates with the Post-Zionist/New Historians that are undergoing a revisionist read of the founding of the state of Israel. There are, as I mentioned above, intense clashes between such ideological tribes and within such clans.

It seems to me if a contemporary form of authentic and genuine Jewish and Christian propheticism is ever going to emerge, a turn to Martin Buber and Abraham Heschel offers some guidance and pointers. Those who are frozen in a limited, nationalist, and reductionistic read of history and the Bible will never experience the spring season of a better world. If we are ever going to update the classical Jewish prophetic way, a middle path does need to be found between an uncritical form of Jewish and Christian Zionism and an uncritical attachment to the "New Historians" revisionist read of Israeli history. We also need to bring to the table the insights of leading Palestinians such as Naim Ateek, Edward Said, Mitri Raheb, Johanna Katanacho, and Nur Masalha (editor of *Holy Land Studies*). There is as much internal debate and dialogue within the Palestinian community as there is within the Jewish and Christian communities on the Jewish statehood issue, the implications of the founding of the state of Israel and the substantive American-Jewish alliance.

There can be no doubt, by way of conclusion, that the Jewish use of the Holocaust and an idealized interpretation of the founding of the state of Israel need to be offset by the Palestinian "Nakba" and the reality of the Palestinian diaspora, the West Bank, and Gaza. If this more honest read of history is not carried out, dishonesty prevails, injustice dominates, and the dove will be bought and sold again, sold and bought again.

APPENDIX V

IRVING LAYTON, ZIONISM, AND THE USA

IRVING LAYTON WAS ONE OF the most intense, demanding, and explosive Canadian poets on the literary stage. There is something in Layton that veers towards the prophetic, but seriously distorts the prophetic in his poetic and literary journey. Layton was a Jew and stood, in many ways, proudly within his Jewish heritage. Layton was convinced that in the post Holocaust world a serious rethink had to be done about Western Civilization, Christianity, and Judaism. There can be no doubt that Layton's poetry seems to have a prophetic bite to it that brooks no opposition as does his prose.

Layton published a poetic trilogy in the mid-1970s that turned on Christianity with vengeance while upholding Jesus as a Jewish prophet: *For My Brother Jesus* (1976), *The Covenant* (1977) and *Dropping from Heaven* (1979) were controversial fire hose assaults on much that was assumed good, true, and beautiful in Christianity, Canada and beyond.

Poem after poem undermines Christianity and significant aspects of the West. The treatment of Jews in Canada is compared and contrasted with treatment of the Jews in the United States (to the detriment of Canada and praise of the USA).

Layton's notion of the Jewish heritage is not a simple one—complex indeed. His inclusion of the Jewish prophets makes it appear that he sees himself standing and writing within such a line and lineage. The sheer compact power of his poetry cannot be denied. The style and content has many affinities with Nietzsche (whom Layton acknowledges).

Poetic aphorisms are shot from the gun of Layton's poetry with searching and hard-hitting implications. Each poem cannot but leave the reader somewhat stunned and challenged, confused and questioning. Layton—in life, poetry, presence, and prose—embodied a sort of prophetic pose and posture that could be intimidating. But, when the actual content of the poetry is probed, what are some of the conclusions that must be faced?

First, Layton was convinced (as are many) that Christianity laid the groundwork for the Holocaust. Second, Layton argued (and did so well and vigorously) that Christianity had seriously misinterpreted Jesus and Paul was largely to blame for this. Third, there could be some affinities between Jews and Christians if Christians reduced Jesus to a Jewish prophetic figure; indeed, Jesus was Layton's Jewish brother but nothing more. Fourth, it was the Americans who played the leading role in ending WWII and freeing Jews from the death camps; this means the Americans are the site of Layton's unbounded favour and adulation. Fifth, it is also in the United States that the Jews are treated better than any other place in the world (and history); again, the United States is held high as the great and good place. The implications of Layton's read of Jewish-Christian history, interestingly enough, although differing with Christian Zionists in some important areas, ends in some of the same places: Israel must be protected, the American-Israeli alliance is an imperative, and the sordid Christian treatment of the Jews and misread of

Jesus needs to be confronted. Needless to say, Christian Zionists may differ with Layton's read of Jesus and Paul's misread of Jesus, but the American-Israel alliance is foundational to their End Times scenario.

I cannot sum up Layton better than Layton himself then in the Foreword to *For My Brother Jesus*:

> One of the functions of poetry is to disturb the accumulated complacencies of people, to make them take a fresh look at the reality which habit and custom prevent them from seeing plainly. In this collection of poems I am out to accomplish two things.[22]

We do know in reading this prelude to Layton's main points some tough challenges are about to come our way. What are the two things with which Layton will hit us over the head with a sledgehammer?

> First, to reclaim Jesus for the Jews as one of their greatest prophets. He continues the Judaic revelation that beginning with Moses is articulated after him by those majestic figures of Hebrew prophecy, Isaiah, Jeremiah, and Amos. It is an historical mischance, largely through the work of Saint Paul, that Jesus has been wrenched from the succession of prophets and turned into a deity that intelligent gentiles are able to worship only with increasing embarrassment. The content of the first point is telling and would be contested by many, but the second point is yet more confrontational. Secondly,

---

[22] Layton, *For My Brother Jesus*, xv.

> I want to de-hypnotize people through outrage, imagination, and truth to an awareness that Christianity is founded neither on myth nor fiction but on an ignoble lie. That lie, trumpeted in churches, cathedrals, universities, mission schools, and Boy Scout rallies has been responsible for the cruel deaths of millions of innocent people by blazing faggot, sword, and hunger: most recently, by chemicals and mass executions. If I am not fooling myself, the note of protest and indignation which I sound in these poems has never before been heard in English poetry or in any other European literature.[23]

The rest of the Foreword continues the fist in the face punching style of Layton. Obviously, Christian Zionists would not walk side-by-side with Layton's theological and political read of Christianity (which he continues to unfold in the Foreword), but the conclusion Layton comes to has some affinities with Christian Zionism: America is the great and good country that has defended Jews and the American-Israeli alliance is a good that must be supported.

The forceful Foreword in *For My Brother Jesus* generated a flurry of reactions and responses to Layton. The Foreword in *Covenant* maintains much the same debunking of Christianity at an intellectual and political level, but in *Covenant*, Layton makes a distinction between Christians (those who were true to the deeper core of their faith and cared for the Jews) and Christianity (that played a historic role in the poor treatment of Jews and the Holocaust). There are

---

[23] Ibid.

many parallels in Layton's writings to William Nicholls (whom I have discussed above).

Layton embodies an understanding of the prophetic within the Canadian Jewish literary and poetic ethos that is confrontational and can be most bewildering. Was Layton a Canadian Jewish prophet? The form and style seems to have some affinities with historic biblical prophets.

Seymour Mayne was one of Layton's students, and in 1996, the publication of *Jerusalem* (co-edited by Seymour Mayne and Glen Rotchin) left the publishing tarmac. Many of the poems in *Jerusalem* are more nuanced and subtle than Layton's poetry, but the multilayered theme of Judaism, Jewishness, and Israel runs through this fine collection of poetry. *Jerusalem* is but a slim missive, but the many poems in the collection speak of many different ways of viewing Jerusalem (both literal/historic and literary/spiritual). The bombastic nature of Layton's poetry does not intrude much into *Jerusalem*, although there are a few poems by Layton in the book ("O Jerusalem," "A Wild Peculiar Joy," and "Next Year, in Jerusalem"). Most Christian Zionists would applaud Layton's poetic offerings in *Jerusalem*.

Often, the writings of Jewish poets are ignored when Christian Zionism is discussed. This book has been on Canadian Christian Zionism, and I briefly discussed Irving Layton for the simple reason that he reflects a way of understanding the Jewish prophetic way (as a Canadian Jew) that, by day's end, has some important political connections with Christian Zionists. I realize most Canadian Christian Zionists probably don't read a great deal of Canadian Jewish poetry, and most likely know little of Layton. But there is a form of Jewish nationalism that shares much with Christian

Zionism (but approaches the topic from different places and for different reasons); the American-Israeli alliance cannot be missed, though.

I began this book with a quote from Leonard Cohen's "Anthem." Cohen is a Jew, but much more illusive and allusive than Layton. Cohen suggests that "the Dove is never free." Is there a way Christians, Jews, and Palestinians can play their roles in freeing the dove of peace for the greater good of one another, the Middle East, and this fragile world, our island home? Hannah Arendt (one of the finest Jewish political philosophers of the 20th century) suggested in one of her classics of political philosophy, *The Human Condition*, that forgiveness is foundational to the way forward; "Irreversibility and the Power to Forgive" (chapter 33) is a must read for those tired of a narrow tribalism. It is in the willingness to forgive that new possibilities ("natality" to use Arendt's phrase) are opened up and the "banality of evil" loses its lustre, power, and insidious nature.

AFTERWORD I

MY HISTORY WITH ISRAEL

Brad Jersak

WHEN I WAS A CHILD, I FELL IN LOVE with 'Israel'—one of the most loaded terms in history. To me, Israel meant the 'children of Israel': the *family* of people born of Abraham and who later followed Moses out of Egypt. Israel, for me, also referred to the *nation* formed when Joshua and the twelve tribes forged their way into Canaan and occupied that territory. And Israel represented the *land* to the boundaries established by King David at the apex of his reign from Jerusalem. Most of all, Israel to me was the family, nation and land which served as the collective *manger* for Jesus, the promised Prince of Peace.

Modern Israel was, for me, a precious extension of that backstory. When I was seven years old, I highlighted Israel on my globe as the center of the world, of history and of God's purposes. I read and rejoiced in the stories of the 1948 rebirth of the modern state of Israel. When I was eight, I listened attentively to news of the Yom Kippur War, convinced that Armageddon was imminent—good news indeed since it would usher in the Second Coming! Those were the days of the *Late Great Planet Earth* and all things apocalyptic. Very exciting from the safety of my dispensational suburbia!

But the Lord did not return then. Nor did Israel conquer my enemies of choice (including the *Commies*). And as I grew up, I discovered the mosaic of Israel was not as simple as my 'end times' charts presented it. A friend of mine witnessed Jewish bulldozers pushing down a Palestinian school (with Christian teachers) while American Christian Zionists cheered. Another friend witnessed the new security wall being built between a Muslim home and the olive grove that represented the family's centuries-old inheritance. I saw pictures of the Bethlehem ghetto side-by-side with old photos of the Jewish ghetto in Warsaw Poland from the late 1930s. Eerily similar.

I still love Israel, whatever that is. I pray for the peace of Jerusalem. I understand and support Israel's political desire to exist as a homeland for the Jews. I understand their national security is contested and that her government needs to respond wisely and justly. I cannot presume to speak to how this should be done, but I do know that according to Israel's prophets, her relationship to the Promised Land is directly tied to two essential (yet counter-intuitive) conditions:

Condition #1: First, the prophets tie Israel's promises and blessings to the just treatment of strangers in the land (Ezek. 22:29), including sharing the land with them (Ezek. 47:22). I now personally know some Jews who believe in hospitality, co-existence and cooperation—those who work as just peacemakers and are weary of those extremists, whether Jewish, Muslim, or Christian, who instigate and perpetuate violence. But I've also encountered those who would seek 'peace' through occupation and domination—who speak bitterly in terms of the "problem of Arab breeding," and the denial of any such thing as a Palestine or Palestinian.

Condition #2: Second, prophets like Isaiah vigorously opposed military alliances with foreign empires (e.g. Assyria, Egypt, etc.). Whenever Israel chose to trust political powers instead of Yahweh for her protection, they *always* eventually experienced devastation and exile. If the Jewish prophets are right about this, why do Christian Zionists promote an American military investment in Israel? If the Bible is invoked, doesn't that foreign alliance ensure Israel's destruction? Or ... if we *don't* believe the Bible is right about this, then why appeal to it when promoting Israeli settlements in the occupied territories or nuclear proliferation for war with Iran, for example?

I finally visited 'the Holy Land' (such an irony) as a journalist in 2012, where I attended the *Christ at the Checkpoint* conference hosted by Bethlehem Bible College and bussed around the West Bank and Jerusalem to conduct interviews with grassroots Jewish, Muslim and Christian peace activists, Palestinian prisoners (many had been beaten, one tortured), Jewish settlers and Israeli soldiers, Christian priests, olive grove farmers, rabbis and the whole range of Zionists.

I met a heroic Jewish sage by the name of Jeff Halper from ICAHD (Israeli Committee Against House Demolitions), who had actually laid himself cruciform across a bulldozer blade in defiant defense of Palestinian homes. I connected with Micha Kurtz, an Israeli soldier during the second intifada, who had co-founded *Breaking the Silence*, a movement of former IDF (Israeli Defense Force) veterans testifying to personal involvement in human rights abuses in areas like Hebron. I supped at the agape meal with Palestinian Orthodox Christians who lamented the shrinking Christian population (2% and ever smaller)—when they could serve as bridge-builders and peacemakers between Muslims and Jews if they weren't segregated and crushed from both ends. I experienced lively conversations with a rabbinical student at the Wailing Wall and a militant settler (immigrated from Chicago) in the West Bank. I wander the refugee camp in Bethlehem at 1:00 a.m. where I was invited in for tea by a young couple, both who had been snatched in the night from their beds as teens and imprisoned without trial for protesting that hideous 'security wall.'

The testimonies of injustice and terror (from all sides) were hard to hear, but all-too-briefly, I also felt some optimism as I witnessed grassroots movements and relief agencies cooperating across religious and racial barriers to plant seeds for change. Christians, Muslims and Jews together, were strategizing for community development, capacity-building and a shared refusal to be enemies. I even witnessed several hundred Zionist Christians (*not* the same thing as Christian Zionism) from Jerusalem ignore the propagandists in order to attend the conference and respectfully make their case for the state of Israel. I stood in awe as the Palestinian college president gave an impassioned plea to see Christ in the soldiers at the dreaded checkpoints, even while enduring the dehumanizing 'cattle run' every morning. For a moment or two, I felt these tiny sprouts might crack the pavement and produce olive branches bearing the good fruit of a just peace.

But my hope and my nervous system started to unravel as I faced the barrage of hate and fear-filled propaganda—as I heard excruciating testimonials of oppression in the realpolitik context of Israel. I had barely begun to imagine the parabolic olive branch when just as suddenly, literal and figurative arsonists were uprooting and burning the hopeful crops, whole orchards at a time. I was heartsick and angry ... how much more so the great-grandchild of the man who lovingly planted that crop.

Further, I cannot understand why any objection is raised to the label *apartheid* for the situation there, defined as a "policy of segregation and discrimination on the basis of race." How is it deniable? How is it even newsworthy? Partitioned territories, walled off towns, separate laws, divided roads, signs to areas forbidding either Jews or Palestinians ... the label is not nearly so offensive as the reality. Maybe apartheid is 'necessary' there ... in fact, right now it *probably* is, since the overarching commitment to mutual hatred seems to demand such measures. Why deny it? But then again, must it involve so many daily, dehumanizing injustices and breaches of the very laws once encoded to protect persecuted Jews? And how is it that supposedly pro-Israeli Christians, in the name of the Bible, encourage the very practices the Bible warns will lead to Israel's demise?

Whence hope? A while back, I supped with a refugee family from Israel. Though Christians, they feel very unwelcome in Canadian churches when congregants learn that they are Palestinian rather than Jewish. I remembered Jesus' words, 'When you did not welcome the stranger, you did not welcome me' (Matt. 25). I wondered how the parable of the Good Samaritan passed so easily over our heads.

I'm clearly at a loss. I no longer see any reason to expect a political resolution. But perhaps we could stand with the courageous peacemakers from all sides by engaging in one simple but very Middle Eastern activity here at home: a shared meal. Before uttering another word of opinion, why not meet and eat with a Jewish, Muslim and Christian Palestinian family over the coming year. Listen to their stories. Just listen. Who knows: a seed of peace planted in our own hearts may just sprout one day.

AFTERWORD II

ABANDONING APOCALYPTIC DETERMINISM IN FAVOUR OF COMPASSION FOR PALESTINIANS

Andrew P. Klager

INTRODUCTION

OF THE MANY FEATURES OF Christian Zionism that make it so pernicious, its ability to trick uncritical Evangelicals into thinking that this ideology—and, by extension, its political ramifications—is part of *normative* Christianity is among its most intractable. Time and again, Christians who were eventually able to free themselves from the lulling grip of Christian Zionism in favour of a more inclusive embrace of Jews, Muslims, and Middle Eastern Christians together—whether Israelis or Palestinians—admit that they previously took this ideology for granted, that they didn't even know they were Christian Zionists. This was my experience too.

What dislodged me from the illusory hold of Christian Zionism wasn't an "aha moment" or even a careful study of and reflection on the theological, historical, and political paradigms that animated my Zionist upbringing. Instead, my awareness of the dehumanizing effects of Christian Zionism—for Palestinians today through the oppression, violence, and marginalization of the ongoing occupation and for Jews in the future who have been earmarked as targets of Christ's apocalyptic wrath—grew out of three intersecting ethical and ecclesial shifts: embracing nonviolence as the 'just' peacemaking ethic that Jesus taught especially in the Sermon the Mount, my Anabaptist-Mennonite studies, and my personal transition into the Eastern Orthodox Church through the Antiochian jurisdiction headquartered in Damascus, Syria.

Reinforcing this more nuanced inclusive embrace, moreover, is the understanding that the settlement of "the land of Canaan" in the Hebrew Tanakh—which Wheaton College Professor of New Teastament, Gary Burge, observes is the only designation of the land that is used in the first six books of the Bible and therefore "preserves an important reminder that the land has a heritage that is larger than Israel's own history"[24]—is always *conditional* based on the compassionate treatment of the foreigner and eschewing reliance on militarism for protection. As Burge again remarks, "To be sure, the nation of Israel is promised possession of the land as an everlasting gift, but this promise is conditional; it depends on Israel's fidelity to the covenant and its stipulations."[25] Elsewhere, Burge is more specific:

> [M]odern Israel must be judged by the standards that the prophets applied to biblical Israel. Today Palestinian Christians in the land, Christian relief agencies (evangelical and mainline), and secular agencies (such as the Red Cross, the United Na-

---

[24] Burge, *Who are God's People in the Middle East?* 65.
[25] Ibid., 67

tions, and Amnesty International) all offer the same complaint: Israel is not promoting justice.[26]

More to the point, as I'll argue below, it is the reliance on human coercive structures such as the military and its *raison d'etat* of violence against human beings that contrasts so remarkably with Jesus' way of kenotic peacemaking.

MY CHRISTIAN ZIONIST UPBRINGING

Underlying my autobiographical details is a question: Why was the theological climate within which I was raised shaped more by family, fellow church-goers, and pastors who were loyal to a hermeneutically dubious and historically eccentric set of End Times predictions surrounding the Jewish possession of historic Israel at the expense of compassion for the Palestinians who endured violent upheaval leading up to and during the Nakba and still today under Israeli occupation? In the cacophony of Zionist-inspired experiences that defined my upbringing, not once did I hear of the negative impact of this ideology and accompanying political ramifications on the Palestinians who already inhabited this tiny sliver of territory in the Levant and who continue their struggle for self-determination, peace, and justice today.

Although I was raised in a generically conservative—even fundamentalist—Evangelical environment, it was underpinned by the denomination on my paternal side that gave birth to the Dispensationalism that organizes Christian Zionist aspirations—Plymouth Brethren, especially the more rigid, exclusive, and chiliastic version of John Nelson Darby. When I wasn't attending a Brethren assembly, I sat in the unfor-

---

[26] Ibid., 120

giving pews of small-town Ontario fundamentalist, KJV-only (with which my parents, to their credit, disagreed), Evangelical congregations that endorsed eschatological fearmongering by forcing the fulfillment of End Times predictions through support for a pro-Israel foreign policy to expedite the parousia, rapture, and Armageddon leading to the destruction of hellbound heathens who were under the spell of the Antichrist (usually the Pope). One such Baptist church had a table at the back for selling fundamentalist knickknacks and paraphernalia, from which I purchased a doorknob sign that read, "In case of rapture, don't bother knocking." I also recall attending a talk by one of Canada's most prolific Christian Zionists, Grant Jeffrey, at a church in the nearby town of Clinton, Ontario and distinctly recall his books, including *Apocalypse: The Coming Judgment of the Nations* and *The Signature of God*, populating our home library. *Day of Discovery*, the Bible prophesy television show set in Israel and hosted by Mart DeHaan and Jimmy DeYoung of RBC Ministries, seemed to grace our TV screen every week if not daily, convincing their viewership that biblical passages that are actually addressed to Jews in the Babylonian exile 2,600 years ago were somehow instead written for 21st-century Western Christians today, that the so-called "ten lost tribes" of Israel must return to the Holy Land for Christ to return and lead his celestial army into Armageddon, and that the Third Temple must first be constructed for all of this to take place, preparations for which—including furnishings and the training of Jewish priests to recommence animal sacrifice and other temple cultic practices—this TV show was very pleased to disclose.

To reinforce this commitment to Christian Zionist principles, the unspeakable brutality of the Jewish Holocaust was used to justify the return of the Jews to historic Israel—at any cost, irrespective of the repercussions. I can, for example, remember my parents collecting coffee table books whose pages were teeming with images depicting the horrors of the Holocaust. This often inspired mournful conversation among family and visiting friends, which was, of course, entirely appropriate had not the Final Solution been simultaneously used to defend the deportation of 750,000 Palestinians in 1948 and their ongoing violent oppression today. Likewise, Christian Zionist impulses often translated into a preoccupation with Jewish culture—from family favourites *Fiddler on the Roof* and *The Hiding Place* to cultivating a fascination with Jewish ritual feasts and Zionist-inspired Christian worship music set to the metre and melody of Israeli folk music, including "Jehovah Jireh" played in concert by Don Moen or Paul Wilbur. Ron Dart's characterization of philo-Semitism in this book certainly rang true in my home growing up. Now, individually, of course, each of these above experiences is relatively benign; collectively, they fortified a Christian Zionist ideology that inspired—and was inspired by—the interpretive grid, expressions of worship, sectarian ecclesiology, and eschatological expectations of my childhood faith environment.

SHIFTING PARADIGMS

My re-evaluation of the Christian Zionist agenda in which I was reared did not include directly trying to erode the foundations of the various individual pillars that propped up this ideology either through study or soul-searching. Instead, my eventual rejection of Christian Zionism initially resulted from my developing 'just' peacemaking ethic and embrace of nonviolence as an undergraduate student. It was only *after* internalizing Jesus' commandment to love one's enemies (Mt. 5:44) that my Zionist paradigm—and its ability to produce, identify, and dehumanize new enemies—began to crumble out of necessity. This paradigm of nonviolence, therefore, universalizes compassion and refuses to turn a blind eye to injustice, either against Palestinians or any others in a position of weakness and paralysis.

As the Anglican rector, Stephen Sizer, outlines masterfully in the documentary, *With God on Our Side*, Jesus' Parable of the Good Samaritan (Lk. 10:25–37) is a case study in universal humanization and compassion. Here, Sizer relates, a Jewish lawyer tries to limit his sphere of responsibility and compassion by asking Jesus, "Who is my neighbour?" Jesus, in response, describes a man who has been stripped naked and is half dead, that is, his identity is obscured by the absence of any distinguishing articles of clothing and the inability to hear and recognize his accent. Despite the ambiguity surrounding the identity of the one in clear need of compassion, it is the Samaritan—whom 1st-century Jews avoided and believed were unclean—who was "the one who showed him mercy" (Lk. 10:37). The primary instructive import of this parable, however, is the need to reject tribalism and obliterate restrictions that encourage dehumanization and instead cultivate universal compassion regardless of ethnicity, social status, or religion. Therefore, my foray into peace theology based on the nonviolent social ethic of the Sermon on the Mount imprinted on me the rejection of violence in all its forms—directly militaristic, systemic, or institutionalized—which today plagues the Palestinian territories under Israeli occupation.

My increasing embrace of nonviolence and 'just' peacemaking coincided with my formal studies in Anabaptist-Mennonite history and theology. This more academic exploration into one of the world's three official peace churches began during my undergraduate studies but culminated in my doctoral work on sixteenth-century Anabaptist origins. What impacted me most is the pattern of rejection, marginalization, oppression, and migration from Switzerland through the Alsace region to the Netherlands, the Schleswig-Holstein region in northern Germany, the Vistula Valley of West Prussia, the late 18th-century colonies in Crimea and finally to North and South America first in the 1870s and then after the Bolshevik Revolution and during the post-WWII Stalinist era. Despite several exceptions—notably during the more affluent decades of the 17th-century Dutch Golden Age and the formation of Mennonite *Selbstschutz* units during the Russian Civil War—these Mennonites nevertheless clung to their original nonviolent principles to guide their responses to centuries of persecution and forced migration or deportation.

Many second- and third-generation Mennonites after the Great Trek out of the Soviet Union have sat at the feet of their grandparents and heard of the austerities, violence, uncertainties, and pain that these Mennonites experienced. Under the auspices of such organizations as Mennonite Central Committee and Christian Peacemaker Teams, Mennonites seek to transform violent conflict globally through development, peacebuilding, monitoring injustices, and advocacy on behalf of those who suffer around the world today in the same way that Mennonites have suffered throughout their nearly 500-year history. Marc Gopin has also identified the source of this empathetic solidarity of Mennonites who "travel the globe in search of the defenseless, keenly aware of their own history as defenseless strangers. In a certain sense," Gopin continues, "each time they work toward securing the legitimacy of Otherness and the identity of a threatened group, they reaffirm the spiritual depth of their own experience."[27] This is true as much for the disenfranchised Palestinians who suffer under a dehumanizing physical infrastructure created by their Israeli occupiers as it was for Mennonites who were refused legitimacy and state protection in the past and turned into refugees whose lives and livelihood were constantly in peril. This comparison between the plight of Mennonites and Palestinians—and the need for universal compassion, peace, and justice that both scenarios share—was therefore yet another indirect catalyst for my exodus from Christian Zionism.

Now an Eastern Orthodox Christian, my empathetic solidarity with Palestinians is not only circumstantial, academic, or spiritual, but is also now ecclesial and sacramental. Around half of Palestinian Christians are Eastern Orthodox, and the birthplaces of several important Orthodox Saints and locations of many pilgrimage sites from Christianity's origin to recent history are in the West Bank. Orthodox Christians who emigrate from the Middle East to North America usually enter parish life in the Antiochian Orthodox Church, which is my own jurisdiction whose Patriarchate is based in Damascus, Syria. Among these Arab Christians are many Palestinians who have managed to escape the suffering, poverty, and op-

---

[27] Gopin, *Between Eden and Armageddon*, 149f.

pression of the occupied territories, among them my own goddaughter whose family used to attend Divine Liturgy at the Church of the Nativity in Bethlehem east of the Separation Wall. These ecclesial bonds therefore expand the body of Christ of which I'm a part to include those Palestinians whose olive trees have been uprooted along with their dignity, livelihood, and familial lineage; houses have been demolished; medical treatment, employment, and family relationships are impeded by discriminatory checkpoints; and whose one faith, one baptism, and one Eucharist unite us in more meaningful and profound ways than mere academic considerations.

ABANDONING APOCALYPTIC DETERMINISM IN FAVOUR OF COMPASSION FOR THE PALESTINIANS

Although extremely suspect by any credible scholarly standards, even if we affirm the legitimacy of the geopolitical signs that Christian Zionists peddle and deterministic predictions of the return of the Jews to trigger the rapture and Christ's thousand-year reign, the actual conditions that regulate this settlement reflect the very catalysts for my own shifting paradigms: nonviolence and empathetic solidarity with those who suffer under systemic oppression. What's more, these conditions—two of them also underscored in Brad Jersak's Afterword in this volume—contrast Jesus' nonviolent, anti-imperialistic teachings and actions. For example, the delegates of the Third International Christian Zionist Congress held on February 25–29, 1996 in Jerusalem were united in their declaration that

> [a]ccording to God's distribution of nations, the
> Land of Israel has been given to the Jewish People

> by God as an everlasting possession by an eternal covenant. The Jewish People have the absolute right to possess and dwell in the Land, including Judea, Samaria [i.e., the West Bank], Gaza and the Golan.[28]

When we consider the Israeli military and civilian occupation of the Palestinian territories, it's difficult to ignore the contrast to the psalmist's condition that "the meek will inherit the land and enjoy great peace" (Ps. 37:11) as repeated by Jesus in the Beatitudes when he counter-intuitively declared, "Blessed are the meek, for they will inherit the earth" (Mt. 5:5). When land is "inherited" through brute force, Christians ought to question their own support of this behaviour in light of the psalmist's wisdom and Christ's example and teachings.

Further, as God made plain in the beginning that "the land is mine and you are but aliens and my tenants" (Lev. 25:23),[29] it is unclear how the occupation of Palestine by Israel's secular government and the Israeli Defense Forces complies with this original theocratic vision. Instead, Israel has relied on disproportionate military strength, funding, and resources to keep Palestinians under its thumb. And yet, the Prophet Ezekiel, whom Christian Zionists rely on significantly to support their futurist interpretations of Scripture, renounces this dependence on violence and militarism in order to continue occupation of the land: "Thus says the Lord God of Israel: You shed blood, yet you would keep possession on the land? You rely on your sword, you do abominable

---

[28] International Christian Zionist Congress Proclamation, International Christian Embassy, Jerusalem (25–29 February 1996).

[29] Cf. Gary Burge, *Who are God's People in the Middle East?* 64f.

things… yet you would keep possession of the land? … I will make the land a desolate waste, and her proud strength will come to an end" (Ez. 33:25–29). This reliance on the sword contrasts markedly with Jesus' way of peace and self-emptying, which characterizes the ubiquitous, indiscriminate kingdom of God that he ushered in to replace the divisive distraction of national boundaries, colonial aspirations, and land. As the recently reposed Metropolitan Philip Saliba observed, "God is no longer in the real estate business."[30]

Although, as David Brickner notes, John Nelson Darby used his dispensationalist schedule to disseminate the view that Jews continue to be God's chosen people and the Church is only a "parenthesis,"[31] the designation of "chosen" only ever refers to the Church in the New Testament.[32] Further, the Church is called to reflect the new peaceable kingdom ideals and virtues: "As God's chosen ones, holy and beloved, clothe yourselves with compassion, kindness, humility, meekness, and patience" (Col. 3:12). This contrast between Israeli militarism and Christ's nonviolence and between the Christian Zionist preoccupation with Eretz Yisrael and Jesus' landless, indwelling kingdom of God is perhaps no more acute than at his trial in front of Pontius Pilate, to whom Jesus declared, "My kingdom is not from this world. If my kingdom were from this world, my followers would fight" (Jn. 18:36). Immediately before this confrontation with occupying Rome, Jesus was of course arrested in the Garden of Gethsemane (now in the West Bank), at which time he was forced to

---

[30] Quoted in Peter Gillquist, *Metropolitan Philip: His Life and His Dreams* (Nashville: Thomas Nelson, 1991), 136.

[31] Brickner, *Future Hope*, 18.

[32] Sizer, *Christian Zionists: On the Road to Armageddon*, 56.

placate Peter's zealotry by ordering him to "[p]ut your sword back into its sheath." Why did Jesus disarm Peter? Jesus continues, "Am I not to drink the cup that the Father has given me" (Jn. 18:11)? In this manner, Jesus exhibits the way of suffering rather than fighting back, or receiving others' violence rather than subjecting others to one's own violence. As Jesus emptied himself to drink the cup of suffering that characterizes much of human existence, may we too deny ourselves, take up our cross daily, and follow Christ's way of suffering in empathetic solidarity with the plight of today's Palestinians for the sake of peace for all of today's inhabitants of Israel-Palestine (Lk. 9:23; 1 Pt. 2:21).

AFTERWORD III

CHRISTIAN ZIONISM

Wayne Northey

"CHRISTIAN ZIONISM" LIKE "CHRISTIAN VIOLENCE" is an oxymoron. Both insights were "coming-of-age" insights over against the quintessential fundamentalism,[33] of my Plymouth Brethren (PB) upbringing. Dispensationalist millenarianism was a PB invention in fact by early PB John Nelson Darby, an apocalyptic Johnny-come-lately in Christian history, though with antecedents. The teaching spread like wildfire along many sawdust trails and otherwise of 19th to 21st century Evangelical worldwide evangelistic and missionary expansionism.

The opportunism of this eschatology "was an effective evangelistic tool of terror to scare people into making decisions for Christ and to stimulate believers to 'witness for Christ' to add stars to their heavenly crowns before it was everlastingly too late."[34] Wilson further declared, "It is not likely that the situation will change greatly."[35] The massive sales alone of the *Left Behind* series by Timothy LaHaye and

---

[33] Historian Ernest R. Sandeen's claim in *The Roots of Fundamentalism*.

[34] Wilson, *Armageddon Now!* 218.

[35] Ibid., 228.

Jerry Jenkins show this to be enormous understatement almost 40 years later.[36]

In 1975 the United Nations passed "Resolution 3379" that declared "Zionism is Racism." It was rightly repealed 16 years later. "Zionism" is surely righteous that provides land-based self-fulfilment to the Jews after 2,000 years of destructive *diaspora*, not least due to past brutal Christian supersessionist theology and related violent mistreatment of Jews that climaxed in the Nazi *Holocaust* and was experienced throughout much of Western Christian history.

Christian Zionism affirms commitment to:

- The Jews as "God's Chosen People";
- The 1948 founding of the state of Israel as fulfilment of biblical prophecy;
- The end of history has consequently been set in motion;
- The Second Coming of Christ is imminent since the founding of the state of Israel;
- The state of Israel as God's declared right of existence for God's Chosen People;
- Israel is key to God's plan in the Middle East;
- There is a biblical obligation to bless Israel.

"Christian Zionists" represent 82% of white evangelicals in the United States who believe that "God gave Israel to

---

[36] See http://www.leftbehind.com/, last accessed October 29, 2014.

the Jews."[37] They appear to affirm the biblical *violent apocalyptic* in isolation from the biblical *just peacemaking eschatological/prophetic*. Christian Zionists affirm a vision of the End Times as Ultimate Bloodbath of majority humanity, not as Ultimate Peaceable Kingdom for all humanity. This vision meshes with *hell* as Ultimate Punishment of majority humanity over against *heaven* as Ultimate Restoration for all humanity. Christian Zionist apocalyptic contains a kind of "manifest destiny" violence like American Manifest Destiny. It similarly affirms Israeli exceptionalism in relation to a biblical theology of peace and justice for all humanity. There is related teaching of Israeli entitlement and privilege that creates misplaced Christian loyalties towards Israel.

This seems the context of Canadian Prime Minister Stephen Harper's January 2014 claim in Israel to the Knesset that "those who oppose the Jewish state are little more than hateful anti-Semites."[38]

Christian Zionism in this way perpetuates centuries-long church violence in the West of which anti-Semitism is longstanding instance. This tradition of violence has aligned with "just war" in response to international State enemies, "just deserts" in response to domestic State enemies, and "just hell" in response to spiritual enemies.

"Zionism" in this sense is the child of the Western Christian European ethos that since Saint Augustine elevated nation and the nation state to God-ordained inviolability.

---

[37] http://www.pewresearch.org/fact-tank/2014/02/27/strong-support-for-israel-in-u-s-cuts-across-religious-lines/, last accessed October 29, 2014.

[38] http://www.huffingtonpost.ca/2014/01/20/stephen-harper-israel-parliament_n_4632269.html, last accessed October 29, 2014.

(Though there is far greater complexity to the rise of the nation state in Europe).[39] Augustine's development of Christian "Just War" theory in the fifth century was over against/end run around the Jewish "*Torah of Nonviolence.*" Rabbi Lynn Gottlieb designates longstanding Jewish biblical interpretation thus in a book by that title,[40] and Jesus' explicit modelling and teaching an ethic of "*love your enemies.*"

Two compelling publications that discuss the North American Christian ethos *vis-à-vis* this kind of violent nationalism are: *Captain America and the Crusade Against Evil: The Dilemma of Zealous Nationalism* (Jewett and Lawrence, 2003), and *The Armageddon Factor: The Rise of Christian Nationalism in Canada* (McDonald, 2010). One thought Canada was a safe democracy. One thought the United States stood in reality for making the world safe for democracy. Both books urgently assert, *Think again!* They stand in the tradition of what the first publication names prophetic realism, a strong biblical motif. The authors write: "It avoids taking the stances of complete innocence and selflessness. It seeks to redeem the world for coexistence by impartial justice that claims no favoured status for individual nations."[41] It is not in the end merely a question of what kind of country we wish to live in, it is what kind of God we choose to serve. Both books aver: the god of zealous nationalism in the final analysis is an idol. One can add: *in Canada, the United States and Israel.*

---

[39] See Cavanaugh, *The Myth of Religious Violence* and *Migrations of the Holy.*

[40] Gottlieb, *Trail Guide to the Torah of Nonviolence.*

[41] Jewett and Lawrence, *Captain America and the Crusade Against Evil,* 8.

Rabbi Lynn Gottlieb similarly explains:

> The issue of occupation and the question of power is [*sic*] important because Israel claims to be a democracy. But it is not. It is a democracy for Jews, but not for Palestinians living under Israeli rule. Israel's system of governance is properly called an ethnocracy.[42]

This is idolatry.

In Chapter Seven, "The Question of Palestine," after about 40 years of addressing this question, Rabbi Gottlieb provides only a partial list of anti-Palestinian violence comprising "The Anatomy of Occupation," in turn of which "Each of these components barely scratches the surface of the tens of thousands, if not millions of stories associated with each category."[43] Her admitted incomplete multiple categories list of Israeli *apartheid* in chapter seven demonstrates continuing overwhelming state-sanctioned harms done to the Palestinians by modern-day Israel. Such stories of violent oppression of Palestinians elicit the saints' cry in the Book of Revelation (6:10): "How long, Sovereign Lord, holy and true, until you judge the inhabitants of [Israel] and avenge our blood?" (Israel was put in brackets, instead of "earth" to make the point). This cry was also indeed that of the *diaspora* Jews for 2,000 years of Western Christian history.

It was as young evangelist for two years (1972 to 1974) on the streets of West Berlin that I began to realize that the old formulae for inducing people to embrace the Gospel just did not work. If "God Loves You and Has a Wonderful Plan

---

[42] Gottlieb, *Trail Guide to the Torah of Nonviolence*, 279.

[43] Ibid., 281.

for Your life" *à la* Four Spiritual Laws by Bill Bright did not elicit belief, *fear of* being "left behind" at Christ's return, and *fear of* "hell" were threatened.

In a life-giving two-year reflection time beginning fall 1974 at Regent College as an eager theologue, a course on the Books of Amos and Galatians by mentors Clark Pinnock and Carl Armerding began introducing me to a whole new take on the *eschatological*. We were to live out *now* Kingdom peace and justice realities in light of their promised fulfilment *then*. I eventually learned to eschew the violent *apocalyptic* through amongst other theologians James Alison who wrote: "The perception that God is love has a specific content which is absolutely incompatible with any perception of God as involved in violence, separation, anger, or exclusion."[44]

This at Regent College was reinforced in early 1975 in an interterm course by Clark Pinnock called "The Politics of Jesus," also title of a 1972 study that we were to read on Luke's Gospel by John Howard Yoder.[45] I also learned at Regent College through Donald Bloesch's *Essentials of Evangelical Theology* (2005) and since that "Hell is not to love any more, madame. Not to love any more... ."[46] Hell is *not* to be *no longer* loved by God. On the contrary, God's "wrath, you see, is fleeting, but His grace [*hesed*] lasts a lifetime" (Psalm 30:5).

Put differently and by extension: *"Christian Zionism"* and *"Christian Violence"* are not only *oxymorons* they are ultimately anti-Christ or technically heresies (false choices/

---

[44] Alison, *Raising Abel*, 48.

[45] Yoder, *The Politics of Jesus*.

[46] Bernanos, *The Diary of a Country Priest*, 164.

ways). They are part of the "the wide, broad, easy, crowded path [that] leads to death" (Matthew 7:13), for "Not everyone who says to Me, 'Lord, Lord,' will enter the kingdom of heaven. Simply calling Me 'Lord' will not be enough. Only those who do the will of My Father who is in heaven will join Me in heaven" (Matthew 7:21). But this is ever humanity's, not God's choice. Only I can choose to enter, or to ban myself from, the Kingdom of God. Heaven cannot be blackmailed and remain heaven as C.S. Lewis presents in *The Great Divorce*. Likewise, God ultimately says to us, "Thy will be done." Violence by definition and by choice rejects the Peaceable Kingdom *then*, to be lived out in the ever existential *now* of salvation (2 Corinthians 6:2).

To paraphrase theologian Walter Wink: if violent Zionism is Christian, *the revolt of atheism is an act of pure religion*.[47]

---

[47] The original quotation is in Wink, *Engaging the Powers*, 149.

AFTERWORD IV

CHRISTIAN ZIONISM: AN ESCHATOLOGICAL CULT

Archbishop Lazar Puhalo

IT IS NO WONDER THAT JEWISH ZIONISM developed; rather it would have been strange if it had not. The holocaust, or as my Auntie Goshen called it "the show," may have been a catapult for Zionism but it was not the catalyst that created it. In a profoundly concrete way, the Christian persecution of the Jews, often encouraged by civil governments, sowed the seeds that produced the Zionist movement. It is notable that, from the time the Roman government stopped persecuting Christianity, Christians began persecuting Jews. The tragic history of anti-Jewish pogroms began in earnest with the slaughter of Jews in Alexandria, Egypt in AD 38. This first recorded pogrom was driven by pre-Christian Alexandrian academics mainly for political reasons. A second pogrom, in which about 50,000 Jews were killed, took place during the Jewish-Roman war in AD 68. The first recorded Christian pogrom against Jews, inspired by St. Cyril of Alexandria, took place in AD 414–415.[48] It was accented by the unspeakable Spanish Inquisition (1478–1808) and the blood bath of the Kishenev Pogrom of 1903. Jews had suffered a foretaste

---

[48] Although episodes of persecution or anti-Jewish rhetoric is recorded from more than a century earlier.

of the Nazi Holocaust for centuries and it was only natural that they developed a quest for the security of having their own homeland.

Christian Zionism, on the other hand, is a peculiar development. One might wish that this movement had emerged from a sense of guilt for the manner in which Christians had treated Jews over the centuries. It did not emerge from that guilt, however. It emerged as an eschatology cult within the Fundamentalist and Evangelical Christian sects. Christian Zionists do not necessarily respect Jews, or even actually care for the state of Israel, rather they are an "End Times" sect that is willing to overlook basic principles of morality and human decency. Christian Zionists will defend every act of crimes against humanity and war crimes that the Zionist state might commit. As an ultra-conservative, Fundamentalist ideology, Christian Zionism is as capable of accommodating real evil as any other absolutist ideology. For them, prevarication, ethnic cleansing, genocide, war crimes and crimes against humanity are all justifiable so long as they serve their "End Times" ideology.

One can certainly understand some specific prophecies in Scripture as indicating that the Jewish people would gather into their own state around Jerusalem. This should indicate the development of a community created for the peaceful practice of the faith rather than the modern secular state led often by unbelieving political leaders that did come about.

The motive underlying Christian Zionism is the concept that the more quickly the state of Israel grows to encompass all the lands, real or mythical, of David's kingdom, generating a third world war, the sooner Christ will be able to return. In a sense, some Christian Zionists could actually be anti-Jewish or Judaeophobic. They would still support the conquest and absorption of all the land of Palestine and part of Syria for the sake of their eschatological delusions. There seems to be a concept in this group that they have to help Christ and encourage His return, as if God Himself had not already appointed a time for this. Prophecy will be fulfilled without our help. It is my view that Christian Zionism is a large, wealthy and powerful eschatology cult, a cult of the "Last Days."

Studies of Christian Zionism are always important. Knowing more about a movement that can so easily accommodate itself to war crimes and genocide, and which would like to help create a huge and bloody war, is urgent. Ron Dart has rendered a considerable service by opening up our awareness and raising the blinds on the Canadian wing of this dangerous ideology. Since this ideology helps to shape the foreign policy of the present Canadian government, we need to know much more about it.

Bibliography

Alison, James (1996). *Raising Abel: The Recovery of the Eschatological Imagination*. New York: Crossroad.

Armerding, Carl and Ward Gasque (1977). *Dreams, Visions & Oracles: The Layman's Guide to Biblical Prophecy*. Grand Rapids: Baker Book House.

Bercuson, David (1985). *Canada and the Birth of Israel: A Study in Canadian Foreign Policy*. Toronto: University of Toronto Press.

Bernanos, Georges (2002). *The Diary of a Country Priest*. New York: Carrol and Graf.

Braverman, Mark (2013). *A Wall in Jerusalem: Hope, Healing, and the Struggle for Justice in Israel and Palestine*. New York: Jericho Books.

Braverman, Mark (2010). *Fatal Embrace: Christians, Jews, and the Search for Peace in the Holy Land*. Austin: Synergy Books.

Brickner, David (1999). *Future Hope: A Jewish Christian Look at the End of the World*, 2nd ed. San Francisco: Purple Pomegranate.

Buber, Martin and J.L. Magnes (1939). *Two Letters to Gandhi*. Jerusalem: The Bond.

Buber, Martin (1948). *Israel and the World: Essays in a Time of Crises*. New York: Schocken Books.

Buber, Martin (1949). *The Prophetic Faith*. New York: Harper & Row Publishers.

Buber, Martin (1952). *On Zion: The History of an Idea*. New York, Schocken Books.

Burge, Gary (1993). *Who are God's People in the Middle East? What Christians Are Being Told about Israel and the Palestinians*. Grand Rapids, MI: Zondervan.

Burnet, Carole, editor (2013). *Zionism Through Christian Lenses: Ecumenical Perspectives on the Promised Land*. Eugene: Pickwick Publications.

Carson, Beth (2003). *Pastor Bob: A Statesman of Prayer for Canada*. Belleville: Guardian Books.

Cavanaugh, William T. (2009). *The Myth of Religious Violence*. New York: Oxford University Press.

——————— (2011). *Migrations of the Holy: God, State, and the Political Meaning of the Church*. Grand Rapids: Eerdmans.

Clark, Victoria (2007). *Allies for Armageddon: The Rise of Christian Zionism*. New Haven, CT: Yale University Press.

Dart, Ron (2006). *The Eagle and the Ox: Contemplation, the Church and Politics*. Abbotsford: Freshwind Press.

——————— (November 2010). Review Article: "Christianity, Zionism and Anti-Semitism." *Holy Land Studies: A Multidisciplinary Journal* 9, no. 2. Edinburgh: Edinburgh University Press.

——————— (May 2012). "The Bible Belt in British Columbia, Canadian Zionism and the Israel Lobby: Letter from Abbotsford." *Holy Land Studies: A Multidisciplinary Journal* 11, no. 1. Edinburgh: Edinburgh University Press.

Engler, Yves (2010). *Canada and Israel: Building Apartheid*. Vancouver: Fernwood Press.

Gopin, Marc (2000). *Between Eden and Armageddon: The Future of World Religions, Violence, and Peacemaking*. Oxford: Oxford University Press.

Gottlieb, Linda (2013). *Trail Guide to the Torah of Nonviolence*. Paris: Éditions Terre d'Espérance (Earth of Hope) Publishing.

Gruending, Dennis (2011). *Pulpit and Politics: Competing Religious Ideologies in Canadian Public Life*. Toronto: Kingsley Publishing.

Haiven, Judith (1984). *Faith, Hope No Charity: An Inside Look at the Born Again Movement in Canada and the United States*. Vancouver: New Star Books.

Hull, William (1954). *The Fall and Rise of Israel: A Christian's Frank Revelation of Jewish Suffering and Triumph*. Grand Rapids, MI: Zondervan Publishing Company.

Hunter, J.H. (1947). *Banners of Blood*. Toronto: Evangelical Publishers.

Jewett, Robert and John Shelton Lawrence (2003). *Captain America and the Crusade Against Evil: The Dilemma of Zealous Nationalism*. Grand Rapids, MI: Eerdmans.

Kaplan, William (2009). *Canadian Maverick: The Life and Times of Ivan C. Rand*. Toronto: University of Toronto Press.

Layton, Irving (1976). *For My Brother Jesus*. Toronto: McClelland and Stewart.

Macquarrie, Heath (1992). *Red Tory Blues: A Political Manifesto*. Toronto: University of Toronto Press.

Mainse, David (1979). *100 Huntley Street: The Exciting Success Story From the Host of Canada's Popular Television Program*. Toronto: G.R. Welch Company Ltd.

Malachy, Yona 1978). *American Fundamentalism and Israel: The Relation of Fundamentalist Churches to Zionism and the State of Israel*. Jerusalem: The Institute of Contemporary Jewry.

Marty, Martin and Scott Appleby (1992). *The Glory and the Power: The Fundamentalist Challenge to the Modern World.* Boston: Beacon Press.

McDonald, Marci (2010). *The Armageddon Factor: The Rise of Christian Nationalism in Canada.* Toronto: Random House.

Merkley, Paul Charles (2001). *Christian Attitudes towards the State of Israel.* Montreal: McGill-Queen's University Press.

Nicholls, William (1995). *Christian Antisemitism: A History of Hate.* Northvale: Jason Aronson Inc.

Nicholson, Graeme (2006). "Freedom and the Good." In *Athens and Jerusalem: George Grant's Theology, Philosophy and Politics.* Toronto: University of Toronto Press.

Pratt, Cranford / Baum, Gregory / Burbidge, John / Dunphy, William / Langan, Thomas / Oxtoby, William / Powles, Cyril and Introductory Note, Alan Geyer (1979). *Peace, Justice and Reconciliation in the Arab-Israeli Conflict: A Christian Perspective.* New York: Friendship Press.

Rowe, Paul (2012). *Religion and Global Politics.* Don Mills, ON: Oxford University Press.

Sandeen, Ernest (1970/2008). *The Roots of Fundamentalism: British and American Millenarianism, 1800–1930.* Chicago: University of Chicago Press.

Sizer, Stephen (2004). *Christian Zionism: Road-Map to Armageddon?* Madison, WI: Inter Varsity Press.

———— (2004). *Christian Zionism: On the Road to Armageddon: The Historical Roots, Theological Basis and Political Consequences of Christian Involvement in the Arab-Israeli Conflict.* Colorado Springs, CO: Presence Ministries International.

Spector, Stephen (2009). *Evangelicals and Israel: The Story of American Christian Zionism*. Oxford: Oxford University Press.

Stackhouse, John (1993). *Canadian Evangelicalism in the Twentieth century: An Introduction*. Toronto: University of Toronto Press.

Watson, Merla (n.d.). *Merla's Miracle*. Victoria: Catacombs Productions Ltd.

Wilson, Dwight (1977). *Armageddon Now! The Premillenarian Response to Russia and Israel Since 1917*. Grand Rapids: Baker Books.

Wink, Walter (1992). *Engaging the Powers: Discernment and Resistance in a World of Domination*. Minneapolis: Fortress Press.

Yoder, John Howard (1994). *The Politics of Jesus*, 2nd ed. Grand Rapids: Eerdmans.

Made in the USA
Charleston, SC
20 March 2015